Is He Mr. Right ... or Mr. Right Now?

Consciously Create Your Love Story

Heather Leah

Published by
Hybrid Global Publishing
333 E 14th Street
#3C
New York, NY 10003

Leah, Heather.
Is He Mr. Right ... or Mr. Right Now?
    ISBN: 978-1-957013-23-7
    eBook: 978-1-957013-24-4
    LCCN: 2022904671

Cover design by: Natasha Clawson
Copyediting by: Wendie Pecharsky
Interior design by: Suba Murugan
Illustrations by: Brian Narelle

ConsciouslyCreateYourLoveStory.com

When life hands you amazing relationship experiences, why bother to make stuff up!

This is a work of creative nonfiction, from my memory's perspective, and while I have done my best to reflect my present recollection of experiences over time, I did change certain identifying details out of respect for those involved.

I have taken inventive liberty to give each of these men creative names that describe the essence of what they represented, the clarity they provided, and the distinctions they taught me along my journey to create my love story more consciously.

I would like to thank the real-life men portrayed in this book for their love and contribution to the expansion of my soul, both then and now.

Give yourself the freedom to re-imagine love and relationships. Come with me as I take you through my journey of self-discovery and self-development from unconsciously creating my love story to more consciously creating the love and partnership perfect for me.

The introspection questions posed at the end of each chapter may open new thinking and love pathways for you too.

My journey involves nine marriage proposals and my soul's continued evolution catalyzed by being in relationship with each of these men.

From Bottom Left Clockwise
Mr. Office Romance, Mr. Mom, Mr. Iron Man,
Mr. False Witness
Mr. Knight in Shining Armor, Mr. Drama King,
Mr. Childlike, Mr. Rebound

DEDICATION

May you see the blessings in each relationship
of your love story journey

Whether you are single and searching for Mr. Right, dating
and deciding if he is Mr. Right or Mr. Right Now, married and
mismatched, or divorced and doubtful about getting back into
the relationship game of love, I dedicate this book to you, the
reader that intends to create their love story more consciously.

May you be inspired to ask more relationship questions
about yourself, your family influencers, and the men
that you choose to date or marry.

May you curiously unpack the media, religious, cultural,
and governmental influences that have shaped your
thinking and love relationship choices.

May you embrace loving and honoring yourself first as the
foundation for consciously creating your love story.

May you love whom you choose to love when you choose to love
them, free from internal and external influences or judgment.

May you always remember - it is your love story, not theirs.

GRATITUDE

I am grateful for GREAT, my grandmother, who was a pioneer for women making their voices heard, making their own choices in life, in love, and in business.

I am grateful for my mom who is unconditional love in action and always evolving her thinking. I am grateful that we chose each other this lifetime and for her enduring guidance showing me a way forward.

I am grateful for my dad who caused my resolve to stop paying unconsciousness forward and catalyzed my healing journey so that I could experience a healthy partnership. I am grateful that he gave me a love for music and a platform to sing and speak in front of people.

I am grateful for my amazing, multitalented daughter. Thank you, dear daughter, for your exquisite creativity, brilliant communication skills, and your infinite loving support not only during this process but throughout our lifetime together. Being your mom is the most joyful journey a lifetime of motherhood could experience.

I am grateful for my eternal divine partner (EDP), Michael. Thank you, my love, for all the weekends you ran our winery alone so that I could have time to write. I am in love with all of you, your pure heart, and your amazing mind. Thank you for your continuous commitment to consciously co-create our relationship with me. I love how we keep upleveling our relationship together.

I am grateful for Beth and her steadfast commitment to ensuring I finished this book. Thank you, Beth, for the countless hours you spent energetically supporting me through the writing and creative process. Thank you for reading all the chapter drafts, we had A LOT of laughs and fun, and it's just the beginning!

I am grateful for Robin for reading early drafts, validating the direction, and her generous listening.

I am grateful for Sossy and her keen ability to listen deeply and ask the right questions. Thank you, Sossy, for all our initial conversations, as they allowed me to hear my thoughts out loud becoming the foundation of the Consciously Create Series.

I am grateful for Claudia Volkman, author coach at Hybrid Global Publishing, for her ability to gracefully assist in shaping ideas and coaching me in writing.

I am grateful for Barry Auchettl at The Vision School (thevisionschool.org) for his course on clearing blocks to authorship, for his coaching support throughout my writing process, and for introducing me to Karen Strauss, owner of Hybrid Global Publishing.

I am grateful for Jill Lublin's publicity expertise, networking prowess, and generosity on so many levels.

I am grateful for Randy Peyser, author, and owner of Authoronestop.com. Randy has an inspirational way with words and keen ability for capturing and articulating creativity.

I am grateful for Brian Narelle, owner of Narellecartoons.com. Brian creatively designed the book illustrations keeping them light, fun, and playful.

I am grateful for the Frederick, Maryland, restaurants that served me coffee while I wrote for hours in their establishments, including Frederick Coffee Co. & Café and Monocacy Blvd. Starbucks.

CONTENTS

CHAPTER 1

GOLD MEDAL IN LOVE

I have had nine, yes nine, men, propose marriage to me, and I have been with my divine partner for sixteen years now.

I have learned through love, I have loved a lot, and I have heartfelt, insightful, and entertaining stories to share.

Although I may not have been completely aware of or appreciated all nine men's contributions to my life while we were in a relationship together, with introspection I have come to realize how each one has made their distinct mark on my love story. In my opinion, each one of them has been a beloved soul mate, each one of them stimulating my soul's expansion in their own unique way. From one soul mate to the next, I learned how to love myself and stand in my power.

As I looked back and reflected on my relationship journey, I wondered how I could have better determined whether the man I was with was Mr. Right. Perhaps I ought to have considered him to be Mr. Right Now, until proven otherwise. Some men I dated had qualities that were Mr. Right material and after asking more questions and experiencing more togetherness, they ended up being a Mr. Right Now. I pondered the questions I could have asked my potential Mr. Rights so that I could more clearly see how they were going to contribute to the continuous growth and expansion of our relationship and themselves.

I contemplated what I could have seen more clearly to determine if he was only to be in my life for a season, becoming my Mr. Right Now, so I could just enjoy the relationship for what it was and not waste my time trying to make it be what it wasn't. It was far more important to me to have the relationship be of substance than it was to force it into some form (exclusive dating, committed living together, married) that would ultimately become untenable. I questioned what my basis was for determining whether he was Mr. Right or Mr. Right Now. Were my choices clearly my choices— or were my choices heavily influenced by a family member or an unconscious belief I picked up along the way?

With no real examples of strong partner relationships to learn from or any idea how to go about creating what I knew in my heart of hearts was possible for a romantic partnership, I chose to go a road less traveled, learning on my own. I have come to call that journey getting my Gold Medal in Love. Even if I had grown up witnessing positive role models of a marital partnership, it would not have guaranteed my marital success. Last I checked, being born or adopted into a family with loving parents does not genetically transfer to the children and ensure their perfect partnership experiences.

Did you know that there are almost 4 billion men on the planet? That fun fact was confirmed by the United Nations back in 2019. Almost 4 billion men that we ladies could possibly meet, get to know, or date. Who in their right mind limited women to only one?

How did it get into my mindset that there was only one Prince Charming for me, forever?

What solidified my thinking that I could only have one husband, during my entire lifetime, then game over if that one marriage does not work out?

Who suggested there was only one soul mate out there for me? (Oh, the pressure!)

What happens to me should I choose to deviate from these social norms and precepts created by someone or something else? What would be waiting for me on the other side? On the other side, would

2

I experience shame, judgment, criticism, family abandonment, or freedom, growth, and a love that was a match for me?

I wondered if I was potentially limiting my own personal evolution by thinking that I must commit to one person for the entirety of my lifetime. Has the progress of my individual growth and development been stymied by the fact that I assumed my family influencers' beliefs? Have the influences of religious doctrines, ethnic customs, the media, or governmental campaigns and tax benefits boxed me into a narrow lane, or have each of those influences supported me in full self-expression inside and outside of my relationships?

There are many religious, cultural, and family belief systems about the way that we, as women, should or should not be in our relationships with men. Like other women, I was influenced by various family members' choices and experiences, religious beliefs, societal norms, and customs. However, when I was growing up and dating, I was not *aware of or conscious of* the key family influencers that played a part in my "choices" in men, nor was I *aware of or conscious of* the many influences that impacted how I conducted myself in my love relationships. Consequently, my love story was more formed by those influencers and influences than I realized at the time.

Like many in my generation and perhaps generations to follow, I was not the beneficiary of a relationship course curriculum, training program, or relationship coach in school or at home. I did not grow up in a fairy-tale family with a mom and dad who knew exactly how to co-create a strong collaborative, mutually supportive partnership. More importantly, I was not cognizant of how much my thinking and beliefs determined my relationship choices and actions that produced my love story results and outcomes.

Why a Gold Medal in Love?

The relationship road is riddled with shoulds and should nots. You should do this, and you should not do that. Whether the shoulds

3

and should nots come from family members, religious text, friends, society, the media, self-doubt, or the judgment in your own head, any one of them or all of them can stop you from having and experiencing your love story to the fullest.

I remember very clearly the specific painful moments of religious judgment I have encountered from those closest to me surrounding my choices to either marry or divorce. I remember thinking to myself, *I wonder if I were an Olympic athlete working to win a gold medal in a specific sport, would they judge me each time I practiced the sport or lost an event? Would they judge me for picking myself up, going for it again, and not quitting on my dream of going for the gold? Or would they keep cheering me on encouraging me to get back up and try again until I succeeded at what I wanted to win and experience for my life?*

If I were an Olympic athlete, most likely my training would take four to eight years of intense running, swimming, and cycling for five to six hours every day. In addition, I would have the benefit of a coach who was positive, focused, knowledgeable, observant, patient, and a good communicator, providing me with feedback along the way so that I could improve my game to such a level that I could win a gold medal in my sport of choice.

My internal commitment to experiencing a co-created, strong, mutually supportive partnership led me to examine my thinking and beliefs, which allowed me to gain greater insight, led me to make life-changing decisions, and enabled me to expand my ability to love unconditionally along the relationship road, stretching myself toward obtaining a gold medal in the Game of Love.

My commitment required me to never give up on having what I believed to be right for me, regardless of what anyone else believed I should think, say, or do. It required me to reflect and gain insight into where I may have created my love relationships unconsciously. It allowed me to decipher and obtain greater clarity surrounding my preferences in men, and eventually, more consciously create a love partnership that was perfect for me.

4

Once I started down this path, I became more aware of the potential influencers *and* influences in my relationship decision-making processes. An *influencer* is a person who influences another. For example, my immediate family, extended family, or friends. An *influence* is something that has the capacity to have an effect or a compelling force on the character, development, or behavior of someone. For example, the influence of television, media campaigns, religious doctrines, your birth order, and regional or geographical customs.

The family relationship influencers can perhaps be a bit more obvious—that is, if you take the time to reflect on them *before* you get into a relationship or as you begin dating someone while you are exploring and getting to know each other. If you are engaged, spending time talking about each other's key influencers might be intriguing and possibly revealing. I will spend more time on this topic of key influencers in Chapters 3, 4, and 5.

When I was sixteen, I can assure you, the last thing I was was self-aware. I was a cheerleader, voted most school spirit, pretty much an average B student, involved in sports, and much more interested in being social. I am confident that I did not spend any time reflecting on what I liked or did not like about the guys I went out with in high school, none for very long. I can't remember several of their names, and my mother use to tease me about changing guys like I changed clothes. Dating lots of guys is a good thing. There is no judgment here. In fact, I encourage it, as your experiences can be leveraged as wonderful teachers, expanding your conscious awareness to your relationship preferences.

As a teenager and young adult, I was unconscious as to the amount of impact my key family influencers had on my relationship choices. I was also unconscious of the many other relationship influences involved in defining and/or manipulating the "Game of Love" rules, like the government, the customs and traditions of a culture, the part of the country a person is raised in, beliefs in religious teachings or doctrine, ethnicity expression and identification, and communication outlets, whether they be printed, published, on the news, broadcast on the radio or television, in advertising, and, of course, at movie theaters.

If anyone would have asked me what influenced my relationship choices at the brilliant age of twenty, left up to my white-girl-raised-in-Southern-California-unaware self, I would have most likely said my relationship foundation was based upon "no one else." That in and of itself would have been an unconscious answer, which is exactly why I am writing. I was unconscious at the time, and I am writing about the journey toward consciously creating your love story.

By the time I was twenty, I had experienced the world of relationships through watching my grandparents, parents, aunts, and uncles, and I learned things by talking with my high school classmates. I was fed additional relationship information from *Teen* and *Cosmopolitan* magazines and fantasies portrayed on TV shows, in movies, or dramatized in romance novels. One thing I knew for sure was that I was attracted to men who were intelligent, honest, had loving hearts, dark hair, and blue eyes.

I was the second child of five siblings in my family and, according to Dr. Kevin Leman, a psychologist who has studied birth order since 1967 and author of *The Birth Order Book: Why You Are the Way You Are,*[1] where you are in your family birth order could be linked to your personality traits.

I have no doubt that my birth order has been an *influence* in shaping many of my personality traits, and as a human being, I am multidimensional and shaped by many other things as well. Way beyond my birth order, there were several hidden influences that molded my thinking and temporarily fashioned my beliefs about what a family composition *should* look like, what my role in a family *should* be, what men were like or *should* be, and how relationships with men *should* be. These thoughts and beliefs had bearing on the choices I made and the actions I took ... and

---

[1] Dr. Kevin Leman, *The Birth Order Book: Why You Are the Way You Are* (Grand Rapids, MI: Revell, 1985).

those actions had results and sometimes very painful unintended consequences.

Some people say that *shoulds* are like shit and we best not should or shit on ourselves or others. If we make our choices because someone or something else said, we *should* do something the way that they would do it, then we are following their beliefs, not our own, and potentially limiting our own self-expression and growth. If we say someone else *should* do something the way that we would do it, then we are trying to force our beliefs on them and potentially limiting their self-expression, expansion, and experience.

As you can imagine, with all the relationship shoulds and should nots defined by all the influencers and influences I mentioned above, I have experienced my share of judgment or "shoulding" from others surrounding my choices to date multiple guys, marry the men I married, divorce the men I chose to divorce, and then choose to marry again. I have even had long-term "friends" in the Church say that they could no longer associate with me in hopes that "withdrawing their love and leaving me in isolation" would bring me back to my senses and my marriage.

Besides a church community running away from me like I was the plague, some members of my family were also not in agreement with my choices and voiced their opinions too. Some of their *shoulds* were written in letters to me, some were shared with me in person, and others were shared with other family members when I was not around to hear what they had to say. Some of their opinions were worth listening to and steered me to look inward and reflect, which made a lasting difference in my life. Some of their opinions while I was in a vulnerable and transitional time in my life were unsupportive and judgmental with a biting sting.

Just because they were family, I assumed that 100 percent of them would side with me on my choices and have my back. That assumption was wrong. Like any other human beings walking the planet, they too have had their share of influencers and influences shaping their belief systems about relationships and the way that

7

they and everyone else *should* behave inside of this **4,350-year-old institution**[2] and convention we call marriage.

I did not grow up in a fairy-tale family with a mom and dad who knew exactly how to co-create a strong, collaborative, mutually supportive partnership. Then again, neither did either of my parents for that matter. Without any real-life examples to watch and learn from, without any "how-to" partnership handbook or roadmap, or any idea how to go about creating what I knew in my heart of hearts was possible in the way of a strong, equal partner relationship that was best for me, I set out on my own journey, had to follow my own road less traveled, and sometimes that road was alone.

You may have heard the phrase "Hindsight is 20/20." It means that looking back on a situation or an event implies that you might have a clearer understanding of the situation, or that you might have insight as to how things could have been done better. It is said that in hindsight, things can be obvious that were not obvious from the outset and implies that one is able to evaluate past choices more clearly than at the time the choice was made.

Part of my relationship evolution is attributed to hindsight reflection. But hindsight awareness means that I always must go through the experience *in order to* be able to look backward and see what I did so I could learn from it. And hopefully, that hindsight reflection would take place before I got into the next relationship. The *hindsight process* takes time. Sometimes years of my life went by before I could clearly see what had happened in the past. But even more important is the lens through which I was reflecting. You see, if I was the same person as when I had left the relationship and had not changed or had not done any kind of introspection, then how clear would my backward-looking lens be, and what value would the hindsight process provide? Chances are I would just see

---

[2] The Week Staff, The origins of marriage: The institution of marriage is now the subject of a bitter national debate. How did marriage begin and why? (Theweek. com, January 8, 2015).

the situation from the same place I was when I was in it to begin with, resulting in no new vantage point or insight.

For example, when I was going through the experience of my first divorce, I initially spent quite a bit of time getting back on my feet. I was faced with searching for a new job, moving to a new city, locating a place to live, and working out daycare arrangements. Single parenting and working full-time filled my days and nights, not leaving much in the way of time for self-reflection or for me to identify the causes in myself or our relationship that resulted in our divorce.

More importantly, I was grieving and not in the right state of mind for self-reflection. Regardless of who initiates the divorce, there is always loss and grieving in some form or fashion. When I did have moments alone, the pain of any self-reflection was usually accompanied by waves of grief, as it felt like a part of my body had been cut from me. Grieving does not have a timeline, and I vividly remember time after time bawling my heart out in the shower, wondering if my tears were ever going to stop. Obviously, when I was grieving, it was not the right time for hindsight reflection, as I did not have the emotional capacity to see through a clear lens.

In addition to crying out my sadness and feelings of loss, there were times that I severely judged and punished myself with a deluge of endless negative self-talk, which only resulted in deteriorating my self-confidence, making things worse, and keeping me in a merciless repetitive cycle. I remember thinking to myself that no one would want me since I had been divorced. But what prompted that? What did I base that self-condemnation and decision on? I even voiced this statement out loud to one of the men I dated, stating that no one would want a divorcee with a toddler. He just shook his head and responded: "For a woman as smart as you, that is the dumbest thing I have ever heard."

A few years later, a close friend of mine, reeling from her second divorce and while in the throes of the grieving process, harshly judged herself by making the declaration that she was *damaged goods* and literally sentenced herself to a life with dogs. She further clarified that she was obviously bad at choosing men and could only have relationships with dogs. Once again, it bears repeating that when you have just gotten out of a relationship, suffering from a relationship, or in the grieving process, your lens could be clouded and not afford you a clear rearview mirror look. This may not be the best time for a hindsight look-see. This is a time for being gentle with yourself and a time for much-needed self-care or you could end up making harsh judgments about yourself or others that will sabotage you from achieving your own gold medal in love and obtaining or experiencing the committed partnership and love you desire and know in your heart of hearts is possible for you.

There were also times when I was in a sad pity-party state where I would commiserate with other single-mom friends of mine, with our favorite alcoholic drinks in hand, and either succumbed to or engaged in bashing the opposite sex. *Oh no you didn't, say it isn't so!* I cannot tell a lie, as there is no doubt that during my younger years, I have spent time with my girlfriends in negative conversations about men that most likely included gossiping about our exes.

While these conversations might have felt good at the time and given me fleeting moments of relief from my pain, they were pessimistic and peppered with victim thinking, further adding to the brain fog clouding my judgment, numbing my awareness, and keeping me from my desired love story. It did not take me long to realize that gossiping with my girlfriends or mudslinging at men was a bad neighborhood to hang out in and was not going to get me ready for the type of romantic partnership relationship I was looking for.

My growing up years, until I turned thirty, I consider my *unconscious years.* I was unconscious of the various influencers and influences in my life that formed the basis of my beliefs and foundational thinking about relationships and my relationship choices and decisions. I equate being unconscious with the fact that I was not aware of nor clued into what those influencers and influences had to do with driving my love relationship decision-making choices that were running my love story.

It is my heart's desire to have a positive impact on empowering women to love whom they choose, when they choose, free from internal or external judgment so they too can more consciously create their love story. In the following chapters, I point out my own significant influencers, influences, and unconscious thinking that got in the way of my having the love story I knew was possible. I demonstrate how my thinking evolved and provide a framework for how you can do the same, evolving your own thinking so that you, as a woman, can more consciously create your love stories and experience more joy and fulfillment in your relationships.

Over the course of this book, I will share about the men I dated, including the nine men who proposed marriage to me. I will share stories and information I learned and used to navigate my own progression throughout my relationships. I will demonstrate how I went from unconsciously creating my love relationships to semiconsciously creating them and finally more consciously creating my relationships.

Let's face it, consciously creating your love story is an inside job. As we change internally, things change externally. They have no other choice but to change because we are different. When we do the inside work, we bring different thinking and actions to all future relationships.

It has been said that the definition of insanity is doing the same thing repeatedly yet expecting a different result.

Let's follow the above logic for just a bit. It infers that I would be insane if I continued to bring my same self, repeatedly, to the dating experience, magically thinking that I would attract a different kind of relationship, especially since the common denominator in every relationship is me.

For example, many women have shared with me that they keep attracting unavailable men or men who are not honest in their communications, or men who do not lean in to generate the relationship with the same level of energetic contributions as they do. These characteristics are not necessarily the best foundation for partnership building material and will never get these women the complementary or equal shoulder-to-shoulder relationship they may be looking for when creating their love story.

In the famous words of Albert Einstein: "We cannot solve our problems with the same thinking we used when we created them."

My real awakening began when I started examining my thinking. The hindsight 20/20 process really came alive and became valuable to me when I went back and examined my thinking at pivotal relationship times in my life. I asked myself questions like: *What was I thinking when I started dating that man? What was I thinking when I said yes or no to each of those nine marriage proposals?*

Then I wondered if the *ultimate insanity* was me molding or shaping myself to fit someone else's beliefs (thinking or thoughts) that were not even theirs in the first place. Perhaps they too were following some doctrine or custom that was written in another era, not relevant today, and they too carried it forward without question "because that is the way that we have always done it, or because our doctrine interpretation says so, or because it is customary."

I wanted to reveal, to myself, what thoughts I had assumed from others or the times my thinking was robotic or unexamined. I followed this model: Thinking = Actions = Results. I worked it multiple ways. Sometimes I examined my relationship results, then looked backward at the actions I took that got me my relationship results, and then I backed it up even further to examine the thinking that led me to take the actions I took.

Revealing my robotic thinking and unconscious relationship beliefs was an eye-opening, hindsight, 20/20 process and allowed me to choose my own beliefs more consciously, shift my old ways of being, which in turn changed my internal point of attraction so I could intentionally take a different me into the next relationship.

To change the course of my life, I knew I needed to create a *personal pattern interrupt*. I needed to focus on taking a different me into the next relationship so that I could stop the vicious cycle of attracting the same types of men, unconsciously piling on more unfulfilling relationships, and recreating an unsatisfying love story.

When it comes to matters of the heart, we need to call out our robotic thinking and raise our awareness to the role they and we played in our past choices. Then and only then will we have the freedom to change the course and trajectory of our love relationship experience(s) and more consciously create our love story.

Introspection Questions

What about you?

1. Are you single and searching for that next relationship but wanting a different experience and outcome than you have had in your love relationship past?
2. Are you dating and deciding if he is Mr. Right or Mr. Right Now?
3. Are you divorced and doubtful that you can trust your inner knowing when it comes to men?
4. Are you married and mismatched wondering what is next for you?
5. Have you "should" on yourself or another person for their relationship choices or experiences?
6. If you don't create a personal pattern interrupt by examining the beliefs that got you what you've had, or do some serious introspection, or examine the thinking that got you where you are, where will you be in a year from now? What will your life be like if nothing changes?

Let's start at the beginning and see who and what in our lives may have formed the basis of our beliefs and thinking today that might be unconsciously impacting our love story.

Grab a pen and check the boxes where the following may have impacted your ideas of love and relationships:

13

Influencers

☐ Grandparents or great-grandparents
☐ Parents, whether natural, step, adoptive, foster, or foreign exchange
☐ Aunts or uncles
☐ Siblings, whether natural, step, adopted, foster, or foreign exchange
☐ Classmates, girlfriends, guy friends
☐ Other family or family-of-choice members

Influences

☐ My sibling birth order
☐ Governmental media campaigns or benefits (Say what? What does the government have to do with it? More than you may realize.)
☐ Ethnic expression and ethnic identity
☐ Where I was raised or lived
☐ Cultural customs and traditions
☐ Religious beliefs or doctrines
☐ Movies and/or TV shows I watched
☐ Books or magazines I read
☐ Radio shows or music that I listened to
☐ Advertisement and marketing campaigns
☐ Others? _____

CHAPTER 2

THE UNCONSCIOUS MASQUERADE

There was not a plethora of privacy in our one-bedroom apartment, so I would walk into our bedroom closet and close the door so I could be with my own thoughts. Once again, my thoughts went to a very dark place wherein I was repeatedly pleading with God and envisioning myself driving at an extremely high speed through the middle of the freeway median so I could end my unintentional life.

Really, God, really?
Does "till death do us part" really mean one of us must die to end this kind of pain?
Is "till death do us part" really a death sentence?
How in the world did I get here?
Why on earth has it come to this?
My God, what's happened to me?

Little did I know at the time that what had happened were two things:

1. At the age of sixteen, during my parent's divorce, I judged my father harshly for his relationship choice to divorce my mother and move out of our home.

2. My uninformed decision to judge him would drive me to unconsciously accept other people's *influences*. Influences like their beliefs about God, their interpretations of the Bible, their opinions about religion, and their thoughts about the way women "should" be and act inside of marriage.

I didn't start out that way. My parents didn't intentionally raise my siblings and me under any specific form of religion; they wanted us to have the freedom to choose for ourselves because they were in the process of their own exploration. My earliest recollection of "going to church" was when I was ten years old, and my parents went to Dr. Robert Schuller's drive-in church on Sunday mornings. We'd go to the Orange County Drive-In Theater, pull into a parking space, grab the speaker, and hang it on the car window glass. Then we'd listen to Dr. Schuller speak as he stood on top of the drive-in theater snack bar, delivering his sermon.

As my mother continued to explore her own beliefs, she soon gravitated toward metaphysical or spiritually based belief systems. In my early teenage years, I participated in an automatic writing course that involved moving into a meditative state and listening to what Spirit had to say to me in answer to my questions. I also experienced being around people who'd spent time developing their psychic skills such as clairaudience, clairvoyance, and clairsentience.

One evening, after singing at a wedding reception with my dad's band, I came back home, and my mom was hosting a psychic reading party. Several people had each placed a personal item of theirs in a large bowl and were waiting to receive a reading from Rose, a psychic with clairsentient abilities. This type of extrasensory skill development enables a person to pick up on beyond-physical knowledge via intangible feelings, much like individuals with empathic abilities do today.

As I watched, Rose gently reached into the bowl and selected an anonymous item, held it up, and began to disclose the knowledge she was receiving as she connected energetically to the item and its owner. At one point, she held up a watch, stating that all she could see was red; she wanted to know why the owner of this item was so mad at another person that they could throw a frying pan at them.

I sheepishly acknowledged that the watch was mine, and even though my mom was sitting at the table, I launched into how angry I was that the other band members asked me if I had met my dad's girlfriend. I kept telling them that he didn't have a girlfriend, but I soon realized they had already met her, and my dad had been keeping it from me.

Even though we were finally able to become a family when my dad filed for divorce and moved out, I still judged him harshly, and at the time, I projected "failure father energy" squarely in his direction. One of the other band members was a deacon in the Church. He, too, judged my dad's choices because they didn't fit with his biblical interpretations, and he did his best to "save me." He frequently invited me to come to his house after our Saturday-night band jobs so I could see his perfect nuclear family (dad, mom, two kids). He introduced me to his daughter and made sure I was at their home on Sunday mornings so I would have to go to church with them. He wanted me to hear the Church interpretation of the New Testament and get saved.

Saved, Supposedly from Hell

And he succeeded. In 1977, I was baptized and became a member of the Church. I was still a teenager, not yet twenty years old, and I was now surrounded by multiple "perfect" families who believed in the strict interpretation of the Bible when it came to divorce: "Divorce, other than for adultery, is a sin." This belief supported and further fueled my continued judgment of my father. I deemed him a "bad role model for men" for leaving my mom and his four children and being with his girlfriend.

My father ensured that we always had a roof over our heads, food on the table, and provided for us until each one of us graduated high school. He never missed a child-support payment and continually increased that child support of his own volition each time his own salary was increased.

There were several Church men, whose names I still recall today, who mirrored the perfect nuclear family role models for men. They, too, had been influenced by TV shows like *The Adventures of Ozzie and Harriet* and *Leave It to Beaver*, shows depicting the stereotypical nuclear families of the 1950s, sold to us by the media, government, and societal norms during the emergence of industrialization and early capitalism. *I bought into the belief that if I became like the wives married to these types of men and as a woman married in the Church, I would not end up getting divorced like my parents.*

I put myself through junior college and soon became the church's secretary, with my desk right outside the youth minister's office. He surprised me one day by suggesting that I go to business school. He acknowledged my business skills and suggested that I go to a four-year college to obtain my bachelor's degree. It was truly the first time anyone had encouraged me to go to college, as both of my parents were self-made and forged their own futures without a formal college education.

Another very influential church leader spent his time working with young adults and couples. Everyone looked up to him, his wife, and their family. If you came from a less-than-perfect family, then theirs was the family you wish you had—you know, the family that you sometimes wish you were born into instead of your own when things aren't going the way you'd like. Not only did he counsel young adults from the biblical perspective, but he also encouraged the young women to read the book *Me? Obey Him?* by Elizabeth Rice Handford, which presented all the reasons a wife should be submissive to her husband to create a godly relationship foundation.

I was still new to this whole church doctrine and the *Me? Obey Him?* point of view when I started dating the first man out of nine men who would eventually propose to me. Let's call him **Mr. Iron Man.** He was a nice guy, had a solid job, and took me out on lovely dates. His goal was to be a deacon and eventually an elder in the Church. He needed a "perfect wife" to reach his goals and expressed expectations that I would obey him, be a full-time homemaker, raise his children, sew his clothes, and yes ... iron his jeans, pants, and shirts, making sure that the creases were firmly visible.

Much to **Mr. Iron Man's** surprise, I declined his offer, to which he replied, "That's what I get for dating someone younger than me," implying that a woman his age or older would understand and fall in line with his expectations. Interesting response, isn't it? He revealed a lot about himself with his response when I said no to his proposal.

If you take the time to listen to and observe the men you date, you can learn a lot about them by examining their reaction(s) when someone says no to them. Do they handle a no by being defensive or do they go on the attack and belittle the naysayer? Are they childish or mature in their response when someone says no to them?

Little did **Mr. Iron Man** know what he was asking for; I saved him from me! I wasn't good at ironing, I wasn't sure I even wanted children, and I sucked at sewing so much that if I made clothes for him, I'm quite certain he'd never wear them in public. During my home economics class, the only thing I ever sewed was a gray sock monkey whose best life was being dragged around by my friend's dog as a chew toy.

A Voice in the Crowd

I continued attending Sunday and Wednesday church services, becoming further indoctrinated into the Church beliefs and strict biblical interpretations while working as the church secretary and completing more of my foundational college coursework.

While there are no specific biblical instructions on dancing or Bible verses specifically stating that dancing is sinful, this Church preached that dancing tempted Satan, and if we were to go the extra mile for Christ, we wouldn't engage in dancing, as this was potential for impropriety.

There were also Church leaders who preached against using musical instruments in the church worship services. To them, it was an issue of salvation; they perceived this to be a man-made practice insisted against in the New Testament Letter of Paul to the Colossians. The church I attended literally interpreted the biblical statement, "Make a joyful noise unto the Lord" as only making that joyful noise *with your voice*. This required everyone to sing *a capella*.

With no instruments in the church, no dancing, no clapping, no humming, and only singing, one Sunday I heard a deep bass voice above the crowd. I asked my friends whose voice it was. They told me his name, and I sought him out. There he stood, with his dark hair and blue eyes, a physical combination that I've always been attracted to. We became friends and over a short period of time,

I learned how smart he was. He was particularly gifted as an engineer, crafted things with his hands, and expressed the purity of his heart eloquently through his writing and poetry.

Mr. First Real Love joined our group of friends, and soon we formed a circle, playing Hacky Sack in the church parking lot, sitting together in the church pews, and forming our own young-adult group. He and I soon realized we were attending the same community college. As we got further indoctrinated, one by one, our little group went off to different religious colleges and universities. Even though he was a gifted engineer, he soon wanted to become a preacher of the gospel and was accepted into a religious four-year college. I stayed behind and continued to work on completing my associate degree.

Turning on a device to make a call, send a text message, or Facetiming did not exist in the late 1970s. The first commercial mobile phone, known as the Motorola DynaTAC 8000X, wasn't released until 1983. Its handset had thirty minutes of talk-time, could store thirty contact numbers, weighed two pounds, and cost $3,995.

While **Mr. First Real Love** was away, we communicated by sending each other handwritten letters via the U.S. Post Office. He wrote me letters and mailed me his cartoon drawings and heartfelt poems until he came home in between semesters. I wrapped up my associate degree, and without applying to any four-year colleges, I packed my clothes, tucked my pillow under my arm, and left with him and our friends to drive to their school.

When we arrived, I walked into the university admissions office. I told them I wanted to enroll in the business program, and I needed their assistance. While they were extremely helpful and worked with me to obtain financial aid, they registered me into administrative shorthand, typing, and receptionist skill-development courses, which was very confusing to me. After a few weeks, I was able to convince them to transfer me into the Bachelor of Business Administration program where I could expand my understanding of business fundamentals in statistics, economics, finance, business, and tax law.

In addition to business courses, everyone was required to take a religion course each semester for two days per week. It was also mandatory that we attend chapel Monday through Friday. The religious expectation was to attend church every Sunday morning, Sunday evening, and Wednesday evening too. Imagine a life where you're exposed to religion ten hours per week at a minimum where Christ is portrayed as being perfect and you are expected to be as perfect as Christ too, amplified. The pressure across campus was real and played itself out with multiple suicide attempts and a few successes.

The university rules included a dress code that was different for men and women. The women's dress code allowed no pants; women were required to wear dresses or skirts no shorter than three inches above the knee. Women's curfews were two hours earlier than the men's. My experience of the Church during this time was that women were treated like children, expected to be seen, not heard, and well-behaved.

Mr. First Real Love and I got engaged on campus, were married by an elder in the Church one summer, and followed the gospel interpretations of the Church for the next several years. We also assumed the traditional roles expected of men and women. I had graduated with my degree, was working in a public accounting firm, and did my best to fit the Church's traditional role, which proved to *seriously not be a fit.*

I distinctly remember sitting through yet another debate from the Church pulpit about which version of the Bible—New American Standard or King James—we should be reading from. The constant preaching of nothing that fed my soul continued to deplete my very life force. I sat in silence—or should I say, I silenced my own agony—when all I wanted to do was stand up in the back of the church and scream loud and long at these men spewing divisiveness from the very book that supposedly was meant for bringing us closer to God.

For several years, I had unconsciously masqueraded as a church wife, when, in fact, I had no idea who I was or what I wanted. I was so far from the core of my very being and true self that I was experiencing my own personal hell.

I was unconscious of the impact of:

- The major parental and grandparental influencers in my life
- Almost twenty years of influences like sibling birth order, TV shows, fantasy romance movies, magazines, and books, along with religion, government, and cultural, or societal norm influences
- My own unconscious self-judgment and the way I had unconsciously judged others
- The influencers and influences on my thinking when I made the choice to get married

In high school, I was a cheerleader and was voted the girl with the most school spirit. I'd been so vibrant, so full of life, singing music, privately, loud, and long from the depths of my heart and at the top of my lungs, and publicly for hundreds and a few times thousands of people. I could dance for days and tear up a dance floor, and I lived a childhood filled with guitars, pianos, drums, tambourines, and music. I was fully self-expressed—until I was "saved" and then allowed myself to be muzzled, culturized, and conditioned to be obedient to something that was actually someone else's belief and not right for me.

I am not stating that I was a victim of anyone or anything else. If I was a victim at all, I was victim to my own unconscious beliefs and robotic thinking adopted from others without questioning them first. I was young and didn't even know who I was. I was vulnerable to outside influences and gradually shifted into becoming what others thought I should be.

Does "till death do us part" mean killing who I truly am just to be what someone else's interpretation of the Bible, written to people living centuries ago, would have me be?

Does the "perfect" nuclear family consist of a father, mother, and two children? This stereotype no longer fits our society made up of multiple family compositions and makes those who don't fit this limited stereotypical mold feel inferior for no good reason and causes them to falsely believe they're disadvantaged. Whether it's our societal norms, media, government, or religion peddling the message, it's still the same message—just delivered by different "drug" dealers trying to alter our perception to their version or belief of a "better" reality.

In a moment of being upset when I learned that my dad had a girlfriend, I reacted and chose to judge my dad's choices. I made a decision that divorce was wrong and then jumped into a religious structure that looked like it promised an escape from the same fate when all it did was kill my spirit.

After six years of marriage, standing in that cold dark closet, asking God if "till death do us part" really meant that one of us must die to end the pain, the pain I was referring to was *the pain of being separated from myself*. The pain I experienced when I became someone who I wasn't, doing things that were not me, to fit someone else's version of what they thought I should be because of their cultural, religious, and governmental fantasy beliefs. I was so separated from my core that I no longer recognized myself. I had no idea how to get myself back, especially if I stayed enmeshed in that religious structure.

My unconscious masquerade resulted in unintentional pain to others as well. Without my recognizing it, it was the beginning of the end of my marriage. You may have heard the saying "When the student is ready, the teacher will appear." Little did I know that my teacher would arrive via my mother, who sent me a book titled *Women Who Love Too Much* by Robin Norwood.

Mr. First Real Love and I originally met in Southern California, and we planned to move back home. While he was looking for a job in Southern California, my sister, who also lived in Southern California, flew to the state I was living in to help me drive my toddler and me, one way, back to my hometown. I brought the book to read along the way.

Ms. Norwood's words pulled me in immediately; as a therapist, she knew my life and I felt she was writing directly to me. As I read the first few chapters, I literally took a pen out of my purse and checkmarked all the destructive habits I had formed that were prohibiting me from loving myself enough to stop the pain of being someone who I was not born to be.

By the time we crossed the state border of Nevada, I was so uncomfortable in the passenger seat of that car, and there was nowhere I could run. There was nowhere I could hide from myself, and my soul was crying out for healing. By the time we got to the California state border, I knew I had no business being married until I could come to terms with my own ways of being that did not support a healthy love relationship or partnership. I knew I wasn't strong enough to get back to myself while staying in my marriage. It could have been my *"Happily Ever After,"* but I did not have the tools at the time to co-create that experience. Determined to start my healing journey, I asked **Mr. First Real Love** for a divorce.

The judgment I projected on my father for his relationship choices was now headed in my direction. My dad wrote me a letter stating how sorry he felt for my husband and said all kinds of hateful things to me. In addition, my church family decided that my "sin" of divorcing was so great that they could no longer associate with me. They truly believed that the absence of their "love" would bring me back to my senses and I would rejoin them.

Thanks to my higher self, I did not succumb to their guilt trip and false logic.

Finding the Way Back to Myself

You never know who will support your decisions or who will judge them. The road to healing may require you to be alone with yourself so you can find your way back to yourself.

Thus, I began my journey as a single mother. Even though I cried for over a year and a half, grieving the loss of what I once believed to be my fairy-tale forever, I erroneously thought I was destined for loneliness. I counted my blessings: I had a good job and **Mr. First Real Love** and I could be counted on to put our daughter's interest first, regardless of the form our relationship took.

One night my daughter and I went to visit my dad at his apartment. She was just a curious toddler at the time, experiencing the world through touch. She was interested in his keyboard and guitar. Everything she wanted to experience, he told her *not* to touch, and if she did touch it, he quickly moved her away and wiped off her fingerprints.

My dad's cup was filled with criticism his entire life. He couldn't help himself. *Healing* and *self-reflection* weren't words used in his generation. His constant criticism of me during my childhood flashed in front of me as I watched him doing it all over again, but this time to my daughter. I decided right then and there that the buck would stop with me. I was resolved to address my own healing as I did not want to unconsciously pass down pain to any more generations. When we hadn't been there very long, I let him know it was time for us to go.

Soon after, my company wanted to move me from California to their corporate headquarters. This was a welcome relief, as it provided the perfect opportunity to change the course of my life, providing a new landscape and canvas to paint on.

I needed a *personal pattern interrupt.* I needed to focus on healing the disconnect from myself. I needed to stop the vicious cycle of taking my wounded self into another relationship, recreating the same pain, and piling on more. I had no idea what I would uncover, but I knew that I needed to get the right support for me.

I "hired" my first coach by signing up for a workshop called Return to the Heart with Bill Ferguson. During this weekend, I focused on walking through a process of healing, opening my heart, and restoring myself. Bill Ferguson started his career as a divorce attorney, and he soon gained national attention for his ability to take the conflict out of divorce and restore the love between two people, one human being to another.

Albert Einstein is credited with saying, "We cannot solve our problems with the same level of thinking that created them." He is also quoted as having said, "If I had an hour to solve a problem, I'd spend fifty-five minutes thinking about the problem and five minutes thinking about solution."

The most important part of problem-solving is to better understand the problem(s) and what might be the root cause of those problems. This process can be further facilitated by breaking the problems down into smaller components.

You want to be totally honest with yourself about the potential places you may be unconsciously masquerading in your life, being someone or something you were not born to be. Identify the causes of the problem and write them down. This process is intended to shine the light on your thinking and assist you in distinguishing whether your thinking is your thoughts or thinking passed down from others that you unconsciously assumed. It will enlighten you to know what you are thinking now or were thinking at the time the problem was initially created.

Introspection Questions

It's important to ask the right questions to better understand what the driving forces are on your love bus that have you continue to create a love story that you may or may not be in love with.

1. What influences have you perhaps allowed to shape your life and beliefs?
2. What strong beliefs of others have you assumed?
3. What fundamental beliefs about how women should behave have you assumed?
4. Where might you be unconsciously or by choice masquerading and being someone or something that you are not in your relationships?
5. What do you believe you should be or should not be as a woman or someone's wife?
6. What duties or roles have you played or automatically believe you should do/be as a woman/wife?
7. What are your religious beliefs about women and their role in a relationship?
   a. Are they yours or were they passed down from an influential person in your life, perhaps a parent, friend, leader, or extended family member?
   b. Do you know how you came to believe them?
   c. Do they still fit you today? If not, is it time for a bit of personal evolution or an upgrade?
8. What is Mr. Right or Mr. Right Now looking for? Is he looking for a traditional wife, arm candy or trophy wife, an activity partner, a submissive woman, someone to travel with, a caretaker, someone to save, a partnership, or several of the above?
9. Whom have you judged for their relationship choices or actions? A parent, yourself, a friend, other family members?
   a. What is your judgment of them? Where have they or you fallen from grace in your opinion?
   b. Where and how can you move on from judgment? What does it look like to change your judgment into love and forgiveness?
10. What were you thinking when you got engaged?
11. What were you thinking when you got married?
12. What were you thinking when you got into your last or current relationship?

13. What thoughts are you thinking now that you are married or in a relationship?
14. Where have you been "culturized"? (Think: cultural and ethnic norms)
15. Where are you still being "culturized"? (Think: Hallmark, Disney movies, and romantic films)
16. Whom have you become and what beliefs have you bought into because of cultural influences?

The next three chapters delve a little deeper into key influencers and major influences so we can distinguish them a bit further.

My major influencers were my grandmother, mom, and dad. As you read the next three chapters, think about the major influencers in your life.

I will shed more light on the beliefs I assumed or traits I learned from these key influencers that were unconsciously running my love story in a direction not producing the results I was in love with.

CHAPTER 3

IN THE BEGINNING WAS GREAT

I'm blessed that I was born into a family of strong and formidable women both mentally, emotionally, and with longevity of life in our lady genes. I have a five-generational picture of the women in my family, stretching from my great-grandmother at age ninety-six when the picture was taken to my daughter who was five years old at the time. I remember visiting my great-grandparents' farm in Iowa when I was in grade school.

I remember being tossed atop bales of hay during harvest time as the tractor drove through their farm's fields and riding on the backs of their horses named Little Bit and Blaze.

I am told that my great-grandmother, Ethel, had a tongue so sharp she could slay the skin right off your back. Ethel raised four children, ran a large farm in Iowa, and could ring a chicken's neck so fast, pluck it, and have it in a pot of boiling water to cook before you had any idea what had happened. She was adamant that in any pictures taken of her, her feet were never to be photographed, and no matter what the Iowa weather, be it rain, sleet, or six-foot-high snow drifts, she would be driven by Great-Grandpa or her sons to get her hair done.

But for me, IN THE BEGINNING WAS GREAT, which begins with my late ninety-six-year-old grandmother, Roni, born in 1921,

31

just nine months after the 19th amendment took effect, promising women that their right to vote would "not be denied" on account of sex. GREAT was the mother of two, grandmother to seven, great-grandmother to another seven, and great-great-grandmother to five. When the first great-grandchildren arrived, we asked them to call her Great-Grandma, to which she replied, "You can just stop at GREAT." We have been calling her GREAT since the 1980s and she was!

In addition to women barely having the right to vote, GREAT was born in a time when traditionalism reigned. This was a time when women were the guardians of "morality"; where the "traditional" female gender role beliefs were prevalent, including but not limited to:

- Women were not supposed to wear makeup.
- Women were not supposed to drink or smoke.
- Women were not supposed to wear revealing clothing.
- Women were to be respectful.
- Women were expected to stay in the house, take care of children, clean, and cook.
- Women were expected to be involved with *one man only* and be fully committed to him ... whether he was committed to her or not.

My mother, my siblings, and I swear that GREAT settled the West in a covered wagon. Most likely she was holding the reins, driving the horses, shooting at someone if she needed to protect her family, and directing the wagon, trailblazing all the way! I have many adventurous memories of traveling the West Coast with my grandmother. I was her co-pilot with an atlas map in my hands (no WAZE or Google Maps back then), sitting in the passenger seat while she drove off the main highways, always preferring the path and road less traveled.

GREAT enjoyed the finer things, had a flair for the exotic, and loved to put on a show. She frequently announced how many shopping days were left till her birthday, would ensure that we celebrate her birthday all month long, and on the day of her birthday asked what time the parade was starting. During the last years of her life, she would still go for her mile-long walks but with a birthday poster announcing her ninety-fourth, ninety-fifth, ninety-sixth year front and center of her walker, collecting accolades throughout the neighborhood as she scootched her walker around the block.

When my mother was a child, GREAT ran a fine-dining establishment serving steaks and seafood. Her restaurant, The Tradewinds, sat on the riverbank overlooking the mighty Mississippi. She also ran the kitchen of the Galveston Island Country Club and moved around the country, covering it like a mortgage. In her younger years, she helped her second husband open the San Francisco, Detroit, and Florida Keys Hilton Hotels and the Galveston Hilton Hotel, where they put in the first indoor pool, which was very novel at the time.

GREAT had a fur coat, a mink stole, silk suits, and in her later days, always wore her gold-embroidered red silk hat with her red feathered boa over her purple pantsuit when she traveled. Many people took the time to tell her how much they loved her flair, complimenting her ensemble, to which she would reply, "Oh, this old thing ... please ... go on!"

GREAT's road-less-traveled ventures led us to camping in Mount Shasta and Death Valley, where we saw newborn deer, road runners, and countless other critters. We also found little off-the-road California coast cliff hangers, where we would park for the night, haul out her hibachi, and cook Hamburger Helper for dinner, then settle into the back of her hatchback car and sleep for the night, waking up to the sun glistening over the Pacific Ocean.

One trip I specifically remember landed us on a dirt road that appeared to be leading us nowhere. After about a mile, we came to a halt to allow the parents of eight little ducklings to cross the road in front of us, ensuring that their family safely traversed the dusty road. Then we proceeded a little further and came upon a secluded river, where we promptly set up camp for the night. Much to our surprise, that river was as warm as bath water, so we did what any adventurous soul would do ... went skinny-dipping!

GREAT was more than an adventurous traveler on the physical roads; more importantly, she was a woman who lived her life true to herself, doing what she knew to do, regardless of whether it was popular, religiously sanctioned, culturally accepted, generationally permitted, or whether she had *ANY* family or friend's approval.

GREAT always lived life on her terms and according to her internal compass. GREAT was born and raised in Bloomfield, Iowa, lived through the Great Depression (1929-1939), World War II and Pearl Harbor bombings (1941-1945), in Detroit during the 1967 riots, Vietnam War (1955-1975), and two husbands.

Like many children, I did not spend much time asking my parents, grandparents, or great-grandparents about their dreams, challenges, or journey during this lifetime. I did not often seize those precious moments to ask them about the wisdom learned from their life's lessons or glean the context of the time frame in which they lived or the overarching influencers they may have been pressured by or influences that formed their beliefs and choices.

A few years before GREAT passed, I got more curious about the men in both her and my mother's lives. I wondered what attracted them to the men in their lives. I wondered why they chose the men they selected. Did they choose based upon conscious clarity surrounding what they wanted for themselves or were their marriages based upon other circumstances or factors? I wondered how their choices impacted and influenced my choices over the years consciously or unconsciously.

Once I started asking questions, the right questions, I found the answers to be extremely informational, and at times heartbreaking, hearing what they had each endured, and in some instances, the answers were highly entertaining!

In 1937, GREAT lived in a small town with less than 26,000 residents where everyone knew everyone. Her parents ran a large family farm and were highly respected in the community. During this time frame, GREAT was a sixteen-year-old high school student, dating one of the high school basketball players whose father was also this small town's sheriff. Like 75 percent of the American population today, by age twenty[3], GREAT and her boyfriend engaged in pre-marital sex. As science has proven repeatedly, one or both of her ovaries produced a mature egg that was fertilized with his sperm, and then she was pregnant with the child that grew up to be my mom.

GREAT's high school banned her from coming to school because she was pregnant, not allowing her to finish her education. However, the high school did *allow her* to go to her boyfriend's basketball games and cheer him on while he stayed in school and finished his studies.

Shotgun Wedding

For those of you who have not yet heard this term, a shotgun wedding is a wedding that is arranged to avoid parental embarrassment and avoid the daughter becoming a social pariah due to her choice to engage in premarital sex possibly leading to an unintended pregnancy. You don't hear much said about the opposite sex and what he had to do with the pregnancy. The last time I checked science, it takes his sperm and her egg(s) to co-create. We can stop paying this unconscious thinking forward, creating unnecessary shame for everyone involved.

The term *shotgun wedding* is an American phrase based upon the stereotypical scenario where the father of the pregnant bride-to-be threatens the reluctant father-to-be groom with a shotgun to ensure that he follows through with the wedding. Once again, we see this extremely old traditional approach where a man decides what is best for us women or "his" daughter, like she is property, by determining that we need to get married, forcing us down a possibility for divorce path just to save face or potentially look good in the moment or to ensure that the daughter does not endure any "disgrace," which is another form of "women-shaming."

---

[3] Premarital sex is the norm in America by Jennifer Warner, 12/20/2006, https://webmd.com – 75 percent by age twenty and 95 percent by age forty-four.

I do not remember seeing many pictures of GREAT with a man. Not that she needed to be in pictures with men, I just remember her stunning self-portraits and have many of them hanging on my walls. I, like my mother, had never seen any wedding pictures of her and mom's dad. I even called GREAT's closest sister-in-law to ask her what she might know about GREAT's wedding day, and she said that she had no idea what GREAT's wedding day was, nor had she ever seen any pictures of a celebration.

I had to find another way to identify the history, so I called all ninety-nine counties in the state of Iowa and talking with each county recorder's office, I came up with the same answer, and that was nothing. No marriage certificate could be located. It was a mystery, and I was not sure how to go about solving it until my new friend Sandy did some research on Ancestry.com and uncovered the marriage certificate.

The reason I could not find their marriage certificate is because they were not married in the state where they lived. You see, not only were my great-grandparents well-respected in the community, but my grandmother's soon-to-be father-in-law was the town sheriff, and he was the law. Both families had reputations to protect, and together they drove over the state line of Iowa into the state of Missouri, where my great-grandmother, Ethel, and his sheriff father both signed the marriage certificate, forcing the two children to get married so they could "save face."[4]

If GREAT was still alive, oh, the questions I would ask and the discussions we would have on this topic! Was she ever happy in her relationship with him? What level of shame was she subjected to? Was her forced husband abusive toward her? Was their marriage doomed from the start because of the forced foundation it was built on? How did she feel about the influencers in her life making these decisions for her? Would she have chosen differently for herself if she'd had other options? What did she think about the influences, societal norms, and beliefs of her generation?

---

[4] Humanitarian, Forced Marriage 10/7/2021, USCIS.gov.

Americans are not the only people who enjoy sex before going to the altar, and it appears that the "women shaming" (notice there is no "man shaming") goes well beyond America. It is a multi-country activity gaining more awareness and, in some countries, evolving, as noted in the organized references below:

United Arab Emirates (UAE)	DUBAI, May 20 (Reuters) – In 2020, seven months after the UAE decriminalized premarital sex, the legal changes in the law were not yet always reflected in how pregnancies outside marriage are treated, according to government guidance, lawyers, and hospital staff. While the law reads women were to no longer be jailed for premarital sex, new births still required the parents' marriage certificate, and health insurers do not offer maternity coverage to unmarried women. In private online chatrooms unmarried women remain wary of seeking medical help for pregnancy issues. If they can't provide a marriage certificate, the hospitals will call and report them to the police and the hospitals will not provide the child a birth certificate.[5]
Japan	The slang term *Dekikon;* translated means "oops-we-did-it-marriage" Many Japanese couples are conceiving before marrying. Of the 569,000 first births recorded by the ministry for the year 2000, 26 percent were to women who had become pregnant before marrying. This figure marks a doubling from 13 percent in 1980. But the rise has been even more rapid among younger women. In 2000, 58 percent of first-born babies delivered to women ages 20 to 24 were conceived before marriage, compared with 20 percent in 1980. Among first births to teen mothers, 82 percent were conceived out of wedlock.[6] The sign of the times inspired the Japanese wedding industry to introduce the phrase *"sazukari-kon"* or *blessed wedding.*

---

[5] Status of pregnancies outside of marriage still unclear in UAE after law change, by Lisa Barrington, Reuters.com 5/20/2021

[6] Shotgun Weddings a Sign of the Times in Japan by PRB 7/26/2002 PRB.org.

China	Getting hitched isn't what it used to be.[7]
	A generation or two ago in China, marriage was nearly universal, and arranged unions were quite common. But now it is increasingly normal to remain unwed: In 2016, more than 200 million adults in China were single, and divorce rates are ever on the rise.
	According to journalist and scholar Leta Hong Fincher, more young people now are resisting marriage—especially women, who she says have more to lose through the patriarchal institution that often leaves them "beholden to a man and his family."
	The Leftover Woman (shengnu) is a slang term used to describe urban women over 27 who enjoy a higher level of education, income, and intelligence, supposedly leaving them "unable to settle down."[8]
United Kingdom	In July 2022, Girlsnotbrides.org reported that 12 million girls are married before the age of 18 *each year* worldwide and are at risk of school dropout, sexual activity often without consent or contraception, and a myriad of health-related consequences. (23 girls married before the age of 18 every minute)
	Child marriage was thriving in the United Kingdom because of a legal loophole. Most recently the United Kingdom Members of Parliament voted on the "ground-breaking" bill in November of 2021 to make all forms of child marriage illegal in England and Wales. Girls Not Brides UK members described this as a significant milestone in their campaign to end childhood marriage.[9, 10, 11]

---

[7] It's Complicated: Chinese Millennials and Marriage 8/3/2018 by Qian Jinghua and Fan Yiying, Sixthtone.com/news.

[8] Chinese Wedding Slang 101 3/17/2021 by CSOFT International , blog.csoftintl.com/Chinese-wedding-slang-101/.

[9] British legal loophole continues to sanction child marriage, by Girlsnotbrides.org on 2/27/2017.

[10] Child marriage 'thriving in UK' due to legal loophole, warns rights groups, by Hannah Summers, 05/04/2021.

[11] The UK Partnership to End Child Marriage, by Maria Fsadni, 11/26/2021

| United States | Out of the world's 140 million births in 2016, about 15 percent or 21 million, were born out of wedlock. According to the Center for Disease Control (CDC) Births: Final Data for 2020 tables nine and ten, *40.5 percent of all births are to unmarried women.* Marriage has become less necessary for women's financial survival, social interaction, and personal well-being, and government policies have been slow to keep pace. Like it or not, out-of-wedlock births are in transition worldwide and create challenges for many societies. Increasingly, single women and cohabiting couples, especially in Western societies, elect to have children and raise them outside the institution of marriage. In many countries, marriage is no longer viewed as the only acceptable institution for childbearing and long-term intimate relationships.[12] |

The reason I am writing about my personal evolution from unconsciously creating my love story to more consciously creating my love story is that I want to see an impact where all women can choose who they want to love when they choose to love them, free from internal or external judgment. For this to be available to all women, it requires worldwide policy and culture changes where women are no longer seen as property and enjoy the same rights as men.

There is so much more country-specific information and statistics surrounding the current state of forced marriages, legitimizing children born outside of wedlock, women's access to healthcare, and other reproductive rights or the lack thereof.

It is encouraging to see the world, albeit slower than desired, move toward a more civil forward-looking society versus an ideological religious society.

Forced Marriage and Husband Number One

At sixteen years of age, GREAT was pregnant, forced to marry husband number one, and, in 1938, my wonderful mother was born. I do not remember my first grandfather being in my mother's

---

[12] Out-of-Wedlock Births Rise Worldwide, by Joseph Chamie, 03/16/2017 YaleGlobal.Yale.edu.

life at all. We lived in California, he lived in Iowa, and I vaguely remember meeting him once on a trip back to Iowa when my older brother and I were in grade school. My mother shared that while her father did not attend her wedding to my dad, he did attend my uncle's wedding to my aunt and my mother noted that that was the first time she had seen him or heard from him in years.

When I asked GREAT why she left her first husband, her side of the story is that he treated her one way in public and another way in private and she could not live with a hypocrite. GREAT once again chose the road less traveled during a time when only 24 percent[13] of women held jobs and earned an income and in the face of being shamed by others, left her two children with their dad while she forged a new future for herself so she could come back and get her family.

Grandpa provided a roof and food for his two children, soon remarried, and did not want to pay child support, so he filed for custody of my mother and her younger brother. With 76 percent of women not having jobs or earning an income during that time, it made it even harder for women like my grandmother to represent themselves. GREAT reached out to her father and told him what the situation was and asked, "What am I going to do?" Great-Grandpa said one word – FIGHT, and then he backed up his words by hiring an attorney.

Husband Number Two

Keith was in the hospitality industry and much like my grandmother, a travel adventurer. They managed and/or opened Hilton hotels in San Francisco, Detroit, Galveston, and the Florida Keys. It was common in the hotel industry to have a drink in your hand and Keith did every chance he could.

---

13 https://canvas.santarosa.edu, Women in the 1930s & 1940s: HIST18.2 - Canvas.

Prior to the adoption of nationwide prohibition in January of 1920, state legislatures passed local option laws that allowed a county to go dry if it chose to. Thank goodness national prohibition ended in 1933 for many reasons, but it is also the reason why GREAT met Keith *across the river.*

Those who lived in Burlington, Iowa, knew exactly what "across the river" meant. Iowa is one of the eighteen states in the United States that is called a **control state.**[14] That means the state has a monopoly over the wholesaling or retailing of some or all the alcoholic beverages, including beer, wine, and spirits.

Burlington, Iowa, has a bridge that crosses the mighty Mississippi, connecting Burlington to Gulfport, Illinois. It was easier for Iowans to access alcohol right over that bridge, and that is how GREAT met Keith, in a Gulfport bar.

During their married life, they owned and managed the Tradewinds Restaurant in Burlington. The restaurant was upscale, had linen tablecloths, and a menu of steak and seafood fare. The restaurant sat on the Iowa side of the Mississippi River and was positioned such that you could watch the cars drive across the bridge into Gulfport, Illinois. My grandmother had a wicked sense of humor, and the reason I bring this up is because she wrote an advertisement that she placed in the *Daily Iowan* newspaper advertising that people could come to the Tradewinds Restaurant, sit outside on the terrace, and watch their tax dollars go across the bridge.

She had a remarkable and creative way with words, always had a crossword puzzle in her hands, with dictionaries at her side, tattered and torn from overuse. When we were little kids, she always loved teaching her grandchildren new "big" words and encouraging us to find ways to use them in our conversations. Words like "unmitigated gall" and "audacity," you know, the usual words you would hear your six- or seven-year-old use in kindergarten or first grade.

---

[14] https://www.nabca.org.

Grandma appointed herself the voice of animals and often shared with us the dialogue the animals were having as she observed them returning from their south-for-the-winter travels, pets circling her ankles for food, or in the wild as we traveled. She always had us in stitches with her voiceover dialogues and we often suggested that she should write a comic strip or a book giving a funnier voice to their barks, meows, and tweets.

I mentioned earlier that my great-grandmother was known for her sharp tongue, using words that could slice your skin right off your back. My grandmother had a similar quick wit. There were many times GREAT would quickly say, "Erase, erase, erase," reminding the entire family that her will was written in pencil and we were being erased from it anytime we crossed her. She jokingly tried to use that as leverage to get us to do what she wanted and the funny ending to that story is that in her last days it was evident to all of us that she never wrote a will, ever.

Grandma was married to Keith for at least twenty-five years, and during that time they lived all over the United States. I have no idea how she used her words with her second husband, but my mother said that she often told her high school friends she was going to write a book titled *How Many Times My Mother Left My Stepdad*. When I asked my mother for examples, she recounted three times right off the top of her head.

I remember vividly as if I were there to witness it my mother recounting the third time. My brother James was six and I was five during Grandma's last stand. My dad was working on Wake Island in the western Pacific Ocean, and my mom planned a vacation, driving with her two small children from California to the Florida Keys.

Grandpa and Grandma managed a Hilton hotel in the Keys where we could order room or poolside service any time, play in the long rectangular pool yards away from the sandy beach, and practice our diving skills while Grandma watched from the sidelines. It was a fabulous way to spend a vacation and when it was time to go home, we had an extra passenger and a boxer dog named Diablo (devil in Spanish).

U-Haul car-top carriers in the early 1960s consisted of a metal box with approximately sixteen cubic feet of internal space and four arms for attaching it to the top of your vehicle. One of these heavy boxes was now on top of our blue station wagon.

My mother said it was unnerving seeing her stepfather sit in his chair with drink in hand, not saying a word, watching Grandma and her pack Grandma's things and load them into the car carrier. With my mom driving, Grandma sitting on the passenger side, James and I in the back seat, and a twenty-five-inch-tall boxer dog weighing between sixty and seventy pounds in the loosely tied trunk, we left Florida to drive across the country to the other sunshine state, California.

The distance between Florida and California is just over 2,500 miles or anywhere from three to five driving days based on the number of hours driven each day. There were no seatbelts in the vehicle, as the first law surrounding cars being equipped with seatbelts went into effect in January 1968 and it was not until 1984 that New York State passed the first law mandating the use of seatbelts for human beings.

When you are in a car with your mom and grandma for days, there are many opportunities for "overhearing" conversations. One very impressionable conversation surrounding the last time my grandma would leave Keith ended with her stating that "You should always own your own home so you can throw them out of it." As a five-year-old, there is no way that I could have understood how the power of that one statement would shape my future relationships and home-buying activities.

If any of my grandparents or great-grandparents were still alive, oh, the questions I would ask them, and the interesting topics we would discuss! They were the primary influencer's in my parents' lives and influencers in my life for the duration they were in our family and beyond their lifetimes.

Of course, they influenced my thinking—just as your key family relationships have influenced yours. The question is how much of an influence? For better or for worse influence? Were their belief's really meant for them and their lifetime? What beliefs did you unconsciously assume that were not meant to be passed on to your life or run your love story?

Introspection Questions

1. How knowledgeable are you about the thoughts and beliefs your grandparents or great-grandparents hold dear? What do you know about your grandparents' and great-grandparents' road less traveled, or did they walk someone else's straight and narrow path? What would they do differently if they could? Can you outline the beliefs that you think they passed down to you and how those beliefs shaped your relationship choices? Which beliefs are truly your beliefs?

2. Are you or someone you know living with a husband or partner that treats them one way in public and another way in private? Did you ever confront or leave someone who treated you nice in public and not so nice in private? Were you judged by others, or did you judge yourself for leaving that relationship? Have you had a chance to examine the circumstances and your thinking when you got into the relationship and your thinking when you ended the relationship? If not, what will prevent you from choosing that type of relationship again?

3. Have you examined your thinking at the time when you married? Why did you marry your first husband? Why did you marry any of your husbands? Do you believe that you came from 100 percent free choice with no one else's influence or beliefs in the mix?

4. As a child or woman of age, were you ever forced into getting married because you were pregnant, needed to do it for the family, or for financial or other reasons?

5. Have you ever experienced being shamed for engaging in sex when you were not married, or being shamed or shame for being pregnant when you were not married?

44

6. As a woman, did you ever experience being shamed or shame for not wanting to be married or taking too long to "get or catch" a husband?
7. As a woman, did you ever experience being shamed or shame for getting a divorce or choosing to remarry?
8. As a woman, did you ever experience being shamed or shame for choosing to be a single, independent woman?
9. As a woman, did you ever engage in judging or shaming other women for any of their relationship choices?

Let's examine and re-examine our thinking. Let's support one another, let's build a network of women supporting women, and have an extensive positive impact on empowering women to love whom they choose, when they choose, free from internal or external judgment. Only by raising awareness to and facilitating the ongoing examination of our own thinking will we be able to create our love stories more consciously, including loving ourselves for a lifetime.

CHAPTER 4

AN OLDSMOBILE, OLD SPICE, AND OVER-RESPONSIBILITY

My mother is an incredible woman. She has unconditional love down to an art form and is loved by many people. With the biggest heart I have ever seen in action, she has worked hard her whole life taking care of and providing for her family. One of her traits that has deeply influenced me is her sense of personal accountability. Not only does she have a deep sense of personal accountability when it comes to family and relationships, she is also over-responsible for those around her.

In the spring of 1938, my grandma was about to turn seventeen when she gave birth to my mother in her parents' Bloomfield, Iowa, farmhouse. Grandma's new husband, Garold, was eighteen years old, earning fifteen dollars *per week* and at the time they all lived with my maternal great-grandparents.

In 1940, just two short years later, my grandma had her second child, my mom's younger brother and only sibling. When my mom was eight years old, my grandmother left her two children with their father. My grandmother saw an opportunity after the war had ended to go look for a new home for herself and her kids away from a husband who treated her poorly. My grandma was away from her children for two years. With a disinterested father, my mom instantly became (even more) responsible for her younger brother.

When my mom was just ten years old, her dad decided to contest who got custody of the two children. Instead of leaving it up to the courts, my grandfather asked my mom who she wanted to live with. My mom's little brother, eight years old at the time, said he just wanted to be with his sister, wherever that was. My mom had to make a very adult decision at such a young age, deciding for them both: They would live with their mother.

One day, not long after my mom had to make that life-altering decision, my grandma came back to get her children. When my mom and her brother were walking to school, a woman pulled alongside, rolled down her window and called out to my mom: "Come get in the car!" Recognizing their mother, the two kids got into her car. She drove them to Galveston to start their new life.

The new home my grandma had found for them was a thousand miles away from Iowa and occupied by a man named Keith, a man who did not want children. Keith would eventually become their stepdad and the only consistent male presence in my mom's life (besides her brother) until she met my dad at the end of her high school years.

Keith, in addition to being disinterested in children, had alcoholic tendencies and a propensity for violence. After particularly bad episodes, my grandma would "throw Keith out." She would lock him out of the house ... then bring him back in ... like they had a revolving door. When this happened, my grandmother would direct her children to pack their stepdad's belongings and put them outside the house, then lock the doors. Then, if Grandma and Keith made up during the day, Grandma would direct her children, again telling them to bring his things back in and unpack them before he came back so they didn't upset him further. My mom used to say that she could write a book about how many times her mother threw her stepdad out, given how often Grandma and Keith repeated their cycle.

The uncertainty and volatility of my mom's childhood shaped her strong sense of responsibility as she acted as a caretaker for her mother and brother and worked diligently to keep the peace to protect herself and those she loved.

Even without these distressing and traumatizing life events, my mom carried a hefty weight of responsibility at home. Since my grandma and Keith owned a restaurant, and while they were away, my mom would take care of the ironing, organizing, and cleaning of the house. When early evening arrived, Grandma often called my mom to come to the restaurant to help wash dishes or take dinner orders. As the firstborn child and firstborn daughter to boot, a lot was put on her shoulders.

In 1955, when my mom was just seventeen years old, she attended a high school talent show where a guy on stage was playing the piano and guitar while singing the song "Hootchy Kootchy Henry from Hawaii" by Mitchell Torok. That was the first time she saw the high school senior that would become her husband. When I asked my mom if she remembered what her criteria was or what she was looking for in a man when she was back in high school, she replied: "They had to drive an Oldsmobile and wear Old Spice." That was it.

To be fair, women weren't encouraged or expected to want or ask for more from men or want more from a relationship. In the 1950s, getting married right out of high school or going to college to obtain your M.R.S. degree, meaning a husband, was considered the norm. When you're a teenager, though, you barely know yourself, let alone know what you want from a partner. I remember dating older guys in high school simply because they had a car, which was part of my unconscious love story creation. Over the years, I have gained more cognizance surrounding the importance of being very clear about partnership criteria. We'll dig into our partner criteria more in Chapter 8.

Well, my dad fit my mom's two bits of criteria! He drove a customized 1949 turquoise Oldsmobile Slant Back, and to this day I never remember him *not* wearing Old Spice.

Just after they graduated high school, during the summer of 1956, my mom and dad learned that they were expecting. Unfortunately for my mother (and her mother before her), birth control was not available whether they were single or married! A decade after my mother's first pregnancy, in 1965, Planned Parenthood of Connecticut won the U.S. Supreme Court victory *Griswold v. Connecticut* that finally and completely rolled back state and local laws that outlawed the use of contraception *by married couples.* In 1972, the Supreme Court in Eisenstadt v. Baird legalized birth control for unmarried people. (See PlannedParenthood.org and Ourbodiesourselves.org, respectively.)

According to my dad's account of the events, my mother was in tears, and when her mother asked her why she was crying, my mom told my grandma about the pregnancy. My grandma immediately drove over to my dad's house and told his mother the news. Their parents quickly planned a wedding for mid-October. My dad called it a double shotgun wedding because both sets of parents arranged their marriage and were going to be darn sure they walked down the aisle before my older brother was born.

My parents got married in 1956. It wasn't until I was in my sixties that my mom shared with me that she knew when she was getting married that it wasn't going to last. Was this a second "forced marriage" in the family? Was my mother or father afraid of the family or social consequences of saying no to a marriage? (For additional context, see the definition and signs of forced marriage in the Humanitarian section of the U.S. Citizenship and Immigration Services USCIS.gov website.)

My mom had two examples of marriage set for her growing up, and a third example that she saw on TV: the "model nuclear family," consisting of a (white) breadwinner husband, two children, and a homemaker wife who tends to the children and happily tends to her husband when he arrives home after his workday. Not only did she feel the weight of responsibility for others because of her upbringing, but television broadcasting added societal weight and pressure telling her to be and do everything for her husband and children, putting herself last if at all.

Seventeen years and four kids later, my mom and dad divorced. Like Keith, my dad was an alcoholic, and he too would hurt his children if they got in the way during an episode of anger. He also struggled with mental health issues, which, sadly, we didn't know much about until later years because of the lack of supportive services and pervasive stigma.

Consistent with my mother's sense of over-responsibility, even after they were divorced, she still took care of her ex-husband in times of need, which she did on and off for the next twenty-five years. Even with everything she's been through in life, my mother has always shown incredible fortitude, kindness, resiliency, and an abundance of inner strength. She is an incredible financial manager and self-made woman. Seeing what she has created for herself and what she has contributed to our family, her friends, her employers, and the community around her is truly remarkable.

However, I can't help but wonder *what could have been* for such an innately good-hearted, incredibly intelligent, and loving woman. What if her primary identity when she was younger wasn't over-responsible older sister and caretaker and, later, wife and mother? What if instead of the family and societal pressure to get married she had had time to explore and discover who she was and what she wanted *before* focusing on a husband or children?

I wonder how much the burden of responsibility wore on her shoulders, as it does for so many women.

The apple doesn't fall far from the tree. I have had to grapple with my own sense of over-responsibility for partners and family, and in many other areas of life that I now realize were unnecessary. It's an awareness that I came to much later in life, but one that has been critical for me in my own evolution as a conscious creator of my own love story.

Introspection Questions

1. Do you have areas in your life where you are over-responsible?

2. Who in your life do you feel responsible for fixing or saving or taking care of?
3. Whose feelings and happiness are you overly concerned about in your life?
4. Where are you suppressing or repressing yourself while prioritizing others?
5. Where are you overcompensating or giving to others to minimize or eliminate conflict?
6. Who are you trying to please or appease so that you can avoid criticism, loss, rejection, disappointment, or potential shame to you or your family?

CHAPTER 5

THE MUSIC MAN

My dad was born in 1936, the youngest of seven boys born to Charlie and Helen. In early 1938, a psychic told my paternal grandmother, Helen, that her son would  soon be taken away from her for quite a long time. My grandmother had no idea what to make of that prediction, as she had no idea how to interpret the information given to her. Just a few short months after that prophecy, my father contracted one of the three types of polioviruses distinguished at the time.

Most people do not know much about this disease today because of the sixty-plus years of vaccine research conducted by Dorothy Millicent Horstmann, MD. Her patience and intuition produced a stunning breakthrough that made polio vaccines possible across the globe. The vaccine was perfected toward the end of 1955, almost two decades after my father was exposed to polio.

My dad contracted the nation's most feared disease of his time. It did not kill him, but he suffered extensively at the hands of others who unconsciously or unknowingly contributed to his traumatic childhood experiences of fear, abandonment, alienation, and tortured imperfection.

There was enforced separation of families during the early acute phase of the disease. Children and parents were not allowed any contact for ten to fourteen days and then only allowed limited visitation for weeks afterward. On and off for about two years after my dad was allowed to come back home, he remembers being picked up and driven in a black car away from his home to a research facility where parents were not allowed. He remembers being poked with needles frequently, and throughout his life, he wanted nothing to do with hospitals because they represented so many painful memories.

Contracting polio left him with a leg that was at least six inches shorter and 75 percent thinner than his other leg. During his early childhood, the doctors condemned him to a life in a wheelchair with a brace on his impacted leg and predetermined that he would never walk on his own two feet. He suffered emotional abuse in public settings due to the cruelty of others who ridiculed or mocked him for his disability, and this contributed greatly to his being a self-proclaimed "loner." But perhaps the deepest criticism contributing to his lack of self-love came from his own father who blamed him and the fact that he contracted polio for the demise of his bakery business.

At the age of five, he found solace in music. Dad got the music bug and learned how to play the piano. During his junior high school years, he also learned to play the accordion and the trombone. Then before he went into high school, his dad bought him his first guitar. That three dollar guitar and my dad's record player were his respite and the perfect combination for the making of a future singer, piano-and guitar-playing songwriter. He was blessed with the gift of singing and he had the authoritative voice of an announcer.

In his early teenage years, he was determined to walk despite what the doctors kept telling him. His resolve drove him to keep at it until his will won out. Even though it was extremely difficult and awkward for him to walk, they soon found a prison where the inmates would handmake his shoes creating a six-inch lift that would enable his hips to be parallel as he walked. As he gained more confidence in his personal appearance and his musical abilities, he entered talent competitions and this is where my mother first saw my dad, on stage.

In 1955, my mom and dad met in high school and along with their teenage friends hung out at the "Hub," which was located next to the theater in Burlington, Iowa. When Mom and Dad were dating, they were frequently seen in his turquoise Oldsmobile, and they were married in 1956.

Their initial home was located on First Street NE, close to the Cedar River, which had a set of outside stairs that exposed them to the harsh elements of the Iowa winters. The apartment was on the second floor of a building close to the railroad tracks used by the American Cereal Company to usher off the All-Quaker Oats train from Cedar Rapids, Iowa, to Portland, Oregon. Dad worked a day job as a draftsman at Collins Radio Company and a night job playing piano as a backup instrumentalist for various traveling musical acts when they came through town, including Conway Twitty and Tony Bennet.

Mom worked in the accounting office for Quaker Oats until my older brother James, their first child, was born. Then my dad insisted that Mom stay home while he was away quite a bit of time working two jobs. Obviously, they had time for some get-togethers, as thirteen months later, their second child arrived.

It was Saturday night and Dad was playing a band job when Mom went into labor for the second time. My mom called some friends to come over and stay with her firstborn while she drove herself to the hospital. Then in the wee hours of Sunday morning, her second child was born, and it was Mother's Day. Mom called her mother and said, "Guess what I got you for Mother's Day? It's a girl!" Having been one of seven boys himself, with a firstborn son, Dad walked into the hospital room, took one look at me, and his first words to my mom were, "What are we going to do with a girl?"

With two children under the age of fifteen months in a tiny upstairs apartment, predominantly alone most of the time, my extremely resourceful mother raised my brother and me and tended to my father while he worked one job during the day and played music all night to fulfill the *sole-provider role* sold to him by the media and other societal norms early in his life.

As a child in our household, I never saw my dad in the kitchen cooking a meal, ever. His culinary skills lie mainly in the grilling department along with his mixology skills and ability to fire up a blender of margaritas. I also never saw or heard him talk about managing finances, as he left that responsibility to my mom along with what was left of his paycheck after he made purchases for his musical endeavors and took care of his car. My dad was not one to allow others to drive his car, including my mother. Mom remembers being pregnant and walking home from the grocery store balancing sacks of groceries on her pregnant hips, with the side zipper on her pants unzipped as far as it could go without them falling off, as they could not afford maternity clothes.

They soon got tired of the Iowa winters and moved to Southern California before I turned two. In his words, Dad was a rebel in high school and ended up not graduating with his class. He obtained his diploma the following year and was more interested in subjects to his liking. He was a self-taught electrical engineer designing the electrical wiring for ICBMs (intercontinental ballistic missiles).

In his spare time, he read books and taught himself how to play chess. During his lunch breaks at the office, he would play chess against two men at time, blind. This is where he would play the game backward. With his back to his opponents' chess boards, they would call out their chess piece moves and then he would call out his moves and this went on in alternating fashion until he beat them both. This only went on for three years until 1964, when American chess grandmaster and 11th World Chess Champion Bobby Fischer played an exhibition game where my dad was one of his fifty opponents. It is fascinating for me to see young Fischer standing at Dad's chess board where the *L.A. Times* captured every move leading to his loss and reading the analysis of each move by chess analysts and enthusiasts across the globe of the game and every move on Chessgames.com. What is even more interesting is that after my dad beat the world champion, he lost interest in the game competitively. I am truly grateful that he played chess with me, as it wired my brain with visionary skills and strategic thinking abilities that I have leveraged my entire life.

In addition to working two jobs, there were lengths of time that Dad would travel for his work. His job took him for weeks at a time to the deserts of California, Arizona, and New Mexico. Then he eventually spent a few years on Wake Island located in the central Pacific Ocean, where missile defense testing activities took place.

While on Wake Island, his announcing voice was recognized, and he was invited to be a radio disc jockey at KEAD, and he played with the locals in a band as he continued to become part of the island's partying fabric.

When he wasn't playing with the band or on the radio, he was hanging out with the guys, indulging himself at the company's expense, which led to all kinds of trouble. My dad described one night when the guys got together and took all the furniture out of someone else's home on the island, replacing it with sand, beach chairs, and an umbrella. On another drinking night on the island, they stole a car and a cannon barrel, successfully cut a hole in the ceiling of the vehicle, placed the cannon barrel on top of the car, and drove it around the island. This was not the first time my dad would drink and drive. It most certainly would not be his last.

When he came back Stateside, to our home and his electrical engineering job in Southern California, he continued to pursue his real dream of becoming a country-western star. He wrote music and played multiple instruments. He was able to get a part-time radio announcer job on the weekends, and he pulled together a group of musicians, forming one of his early bands.

It was common to have what my parents called "hootenannies" at our home over the weekends. A hootenanny is an informal music gathering. This is where musicians and neighbors would come and go until the early hours of the morning, bringing food, playing instruments, and drinking alcohol. This is also where I learned to gauge my dad's alcohol tolerance. During the first few hours of the late afternoon, I could ask him for extra money or something I wanted because, after a few drinks, he was in a good easy-going mood. I learned to sing at a young age and, occasionally, he would allow me to sing one song and share the stage with him. As the evening went on, he would pretty much command the stage and the audience's attention, but after too many people and too much alcohol, he would disappear without a word to anyone, leaving my mom with all the guests and cleanup. Then around 11:00 a.m. on Sunday, it would start again.

There were times that I would come home from school and open the garage door and there he would be, looking like he was dead, seated in the front seat of the car. As I drew closer, I could see that he was only sleeping off the alcohol from the bar he had just come from.

Through our junior high and early high school years I remember the times he got mentally, physically, and emotionally abusive with me or my older brother. It was not a safe environment, and we walked around on eggshells so as not to disturb the August-born Leo lion. He wiped our fingerprints off things we touched, he pointed out the blades of grass we missed when mowing the lawn, he hit us with his hands or his belt, and there were times that he would whole body wrestle us to the ground or shove our heads into a wall.

When he drank excessively, beyond the initial feel-good buzz, he spewed venom on paper. He would take pen in hand and write all kinds of what we called "hate mail," and then he would mail those letters, causing even more pain than what he had already inflicted. He would say and write horrible things about us children to my mother.

My older brother and I laugh about it now, but we used to sing a song by Frank Sinatra to the tune of "Home on the Range," but we changed the words to "Home home is deranged, where nobody wants to play, where seldom is heard an encouraging word, and all you want to do is move away." But my father would be the first to leave—not like he hadn't been gone for long periods of time before, but this time it was going to be for good.

I clearly remember the night he came to tell me. I was in my bedroom, and he asked if we could talk, and since I was in my early teenage years, I thought that he was going to explain the "birds and the bees." This is generally the occasion in most children's lives when their parents explain what sexual relationships are and how babies are made. But the conversation took an unexpected turn when he said that he and Mom were getting a divorce and that he was moving out.

I was in shock, young and uninformed, and targeted my judgment at him. I was too young to know that for the most part, it takes two to tango, both parties play part in the marriage relationship and the marriage dissolution, and if honest and self-aware, both parties will admit what they contributed to the relationship ending.

All I could think about was *You too!* I lumped my dad in with all the other negative role models on his side of the family. With Dad being the youngest of seven boys, he had several brothers before him that were *not* the kind of role models one should imitate.

One brother's wife was a nurse, working two jobs putting him through law school. She came home one day in-between shifts only to find him in their bed with another woman. Another brother was the vice president of a bank. He left my aunt, my aunt's mother, and his nine children, cleaning out all their savings accounts on his way out the door.

Our extended family always discussed the "great relationship" my parents had in comparison to his siblings. Well, it was "great" if my mom did what *he* wanted or if he felt like she was supporting *his* dreams. When she aspired to grow herself and go into the workforce, he was not in support of her expansion. The world and our family were not revolving around him, so he used that as his reason for divorcing my mom. My dad truly blessed us with his leaving.

Broken Family?

Which brings me to the phrase *broken family.*

I have listened to many people throw this phrase around, repeating it unconsciously. According to Merriam-Webster.com, the definition of a broken home is "a family in which the parents have divorced" and according to Reference.com, "a broken family is a family that has split or separated due to a variety of reasons leading to children being raised by single parents, stepparents or others not related to the biological parents."

Many people throw the phrase broken family around and attribute it to a family that is *not* a nuclear family comprised of one dad, one mom, and two children. They mistakenly state or infer that when a divorce happens, the children come from a "broken family." Then they proceed to express the fact that they feel sorry for the "poor children" and project "broken family-ness" onto others just because their parents chose not to be married to each other any longer. We can become more conscious in our terminology by stating "children with parents who live in different households."

In our family's case, as it is with other families, it was **broken during the time we stayed together**. My father's inner child was so wounded from the effects of polio and verbal and mental abuse. He was tormented internally, and the alcohol magnified it. My mom and her four children were collateral damage, left believing that it was we who were not perfect or good enough. After my dad left, it was like someone surgically removed the disease from our home. We were free to breathe without criticism, free to move without fear of being hit, and free to start healing and recovering ourselves. We were given the opportunity to be a family with peace in our home while dad went on to pursue his musical dreams.

The fun thing Dad and I had in common was our shared love of music. We had a music room in our house complete with an extensive album collection and state-of-the art turntable and speakers. I taught myself how to sing, spending hours in the music room playing Barbra Streisand albums over and over until I could hit every note she sang with the same power and duration as Ms. Streisand. This self-developed skill got me time with my dad and the opportunity to take the stage with him and sing in front of people.

It wasn't too long after Dad moved out that he formed a band where country and pop music intersected and named it the Crossroads. The band played all over Southern California at weddings, clubs, parties, festivals, and bars. Dad was center stage with his guitar and attention-commanding voice. I was the only female vocalist in the band. For the most part, I sat in silence on the sidelines until he allowed me to sing one song per forty-five-minute set.

Dad also dictated the way he wanted me to sing and the songs I sang, including Patsy Cline's "Crazy" and "Walking After Midnight" along with Tammy Wynette's "Stand by Your Man" and "D-I-V-O-R-C-E." Since I was only singing about three minutes every forty-five-minute set, there was time in-between when people at the venue, with their drinks in hand came to voice their thoughts. It is interesting that just because you are on a stage providing entertainment, people think that it gives them the right to comment and speak their mind to you without your consent. Even as a teenager, I was surprised by this behavior. I was taken aback by the number of married men who thought it was okay to place their phone numbers in my hand or think that it was okay to tell me how I should change the way I look, dress on stage, or wear my hair. I am also glad that I was strong enough to walk away from them. I distinctly remember thinking that the music business was not a safe place and that if I kept singing these classic country-western lyrics, I would end up just like my dad and resemble the songs I was singing.

By the time I was twenty, my dad admitted himself into a mental health facility. I was the only one who came to see him, and I felt powerless when I did. I remember the derogatory things he said about people whom he felt did not support him, and I can still see the straitjacket they bound him in to keep him from harming himself. It is very traumatic to see a parent in this condition, and I was certainly not prepared to handle or trained to deal with this type of life event, but then, seriously, is any child?

Like so many other things in his life, my dad was a survivor. He was determined that he would beat this too. After he was released, he continued to pursue his musical and voice endeavors. He soon landed a volunteer position announcing for the famous Crystal Cathedral along with becoming an understudy for Thurl Ravenscroft, the booming voice behind Kellogg's Frosted Flakes' original Tony the Tiger.

No matter what achievement he conquered, or how far he reached, his true dreams for fame never manifested further, which contributed to his continued depression, which in turn caused him to self-medicate with more alcohol. This further compounded his internalization of failure, and multiple times over the course of his life, he wrote suicide notes, left voice messages that he was going to commit suicide, or sent me threatening text messages about taking his life.

During my dad's and his dad's generation, there was so much fear and extreme stigma surrounding mental health. It wasn't discussed. In the 1950s, mental institutions regularly performed lobotomies, which involved surgically removing part of the frontal lobe of the brain. The frontal lobe is responsible for a person's emotions, personality, and reasoning skills. Unfortunately, back then, individuals experiencing mental health challenges were considered "lunatics" and "defective" and were sent off to asylums, as "insanity" was thought to be incurable and there was no incentive to cure it—bottom line, during my father's time, we were an uneducated and unaware society.

Here we are, sixty years later, with neuroscientists making advances in understanding how the brain works, how biomarkers measure cognitive function, how nutrition makes a difference, and we now provide virtual access to therapy, health coaching, and meditation as mainstream overall healthcare.

We have Bruce D. Perry, MD, PhD, and Oprah Winfrey's books encouraging us to stop saying, "What's wrong with you?" and start asking, "What happened to you?" so that we understand the childhood trauma following us and others and so we more consciously take charge of our lives and begin the healing process.

With my own introspection process surrounding "What happened to me," I came to understand that my father was not well. I saw that I kept expecting my unwell father to be a "traditional role-model father" and given my father's state of mind, my expectation was unrealistic. Once I stopped "shoulding" on my father, I was able to develop a more realistic relationship with him.

I also was able to see the ways in which I internalized things and created disempowering interpretations that were not in my best interest. I discovered that I had internalized my father's criticism and literally chewed on myself by biting my nails. I could see where I assumed that his voice was more important than mine when he took center stage for 93 percent of each forty-five minutes of music we played while I sat on the side of the stage until it was time for me to sing my song. I had also absorbed some of his mental, physical, and emotional abuse as he paid it forward to our family.

Out of my commitment to consciously creating and experiencing a healthy partnership, it was critical for me to work through my own childhood trauma. I have healed much of it and recognize when my old patterns raise their ugly heads.

Victim of My Parents?

Some people love the melody of a song, some people love the harmony in a song, and because of the art form of storytelling, I have always been in love with lyrics. One song that rings true for me is "Get Over It" by the Eagles. It tells the story of people who spend time feeling sorry for themselves, pointing their fingers at everybody else, being a victim of this and a victim of that. The song goes on, revealing how some victims wear their story like a crown to get payoffs in the form of cash or complain about the present while blaming it on the past suggesting that we get over it, get over it, cuz the big bad world doesn't owe us a thing!

Nowhere, absolutely nowhere, on either of my parents' birth certificates does it say that they owe me or my siblings anything. They don't owe me an education, they don't owe me financial wealth, they don't owe me my health, and they don't owe me a happy childhood. While people, religions, and society have prescribed and created many stories about the way the parents should or should not be, at the end of the day they are just that, stories and shoulds.

While many parents strive to provide for their children to the best of their ability, they will judge themselves as good or bad parents in comparison to the social and religious "shoulds" and expectations placed upon them. All my birth certificate denotes is the name(s) of those who physically gave birth to me, and if I believe in God, then I would take the time to see the beauty in God's design for my life and embrace why God designed my birth through these parents or adoptive parents and family.

The Power of Choice and Choosing Powerfully

It is my life. I get to choose how I interpret my life events. It is *my love story* after all. I get to tell my story disempowering myself or empowering myself. I can create disempowering interpretations that portray me as a helpless victim, or I can create empowering interpretations that strengthen me and enable my forward motion. I chose not to stay the victim of my family or relationship story. I embraced seeing things differently and changed my interpretation.

You may have heard the saying "Hurt people hurt people." I could keep my life focused on the things my father did to hurt us and wallow in the past events, feeding a victim mentality, with the risk of paying it forward to my child and future relationships. I decided to explore owning my dad as the perfect parent for me. I asked myself the question, "Why would I or God have picked him to be my parent?" What might I gain if I looked at the relationship from that point of view? The point of view is called CHOICE. I might ask myself why did I choose him to be one of my parents? What value has his life contributed to mine? Who have I become because I chose him? My viewpoint altered and the following revealed itself:

- Because of him, I have determination. That character trait has enabled me to finish college and transcend difficult circumstances throughout my life.
- Because of him, I learned how to play chess, which developed my ability to think strategically, think ahead, not rush my decisions, weigh, and visually see all the options played out, including the potential consequences of my choices.

64

- Because of him, I was afforded the opportunity to love and appreciate all kinds of music, sing, and be comfortable in my own skin on stage and speaking in front of others.
- Because of him, I learned to pay attention to details others might not see, which prepared me to work in multiple industries and in several foreign countries, leading large complex enterprise initiatives and producing women's conferences and retreats.

Abuse in all forms and mental health challenges are real, and I am not minimizing any of those. I was able to find a way to stop perpetuating my victim thinking and disempowering story surrounding a key influencer in my life. My role models may not have been perfect, but I was able to see the perfection in them because I chose to create a more empowering version of my experience.

Introspection Questions

It's your life, it's your choice, and it is your story to empower or disempower. More importantly, you don't want any old story from your past, getting in the way of the true partnership and love relationship you desire. You might consider playing with reinterpreting, upgrading, and upleveling that story into a more empowering version.

1. Start with something easy: Identify a negative story that you repeat to yourself or others about a key influencer, one of the parents in your life, or a man that you dated or married.
2. Write the incident down (what happened to you) that catalyzed the disempowering story.
   a. Make up a different interpretation so that you have another version of your story that could be less disempowering.
   b. Make up another interpretation so that you have another version of your story that could be more empowering.
   c. Make up yet another interpretation so that you have another version of your story that is even more empowering.

Chapters 6 through 10 are about the memorable men who contributed to my love story, soul mates that caused my soul to expand on my love story journey.

Although I may not have been completely aware of or appreciated all nine men's contributions to my life and love story while we were in a relationship together, with introspection I have come to realize how each one has made their distinct mark. In my opinion, each one of them has been a beloved soul mate, each one of them stimulating my soul's expansion in their own unique way.

CHAPTER 6

WALK FAST—NO, RUN!

We had only been dating for three months when it became clear to me that **Mr. Drama King** planned every move as though he were a scriptwriter for Hallmark movies. Four weeks earlier, I had received an intriguing formal  invitation from him. It was set on heavyweight card stock, professionally handwritten using calligraphy, and sealed with his custom monogram wax stamp.

That day, I was ready to venture out as usual on my early-morning walk. There were usually no signs of life in the neighborhood at this time of day, although a few homes had their kitchen lights on, holding the promise of coffee brewing.

There had been no knock at my door, and I didn't hear any cars or people on the street in front of my house. That made it more mysterious when I opened my front door, ready to bolt out, and saw the elegant envelope in front of me on the welcome mat. When was he here? Did he drive across town late last night or earlier this morning to drop that invitation at my door?

The invitation requested my presence for an evening of dinner, theater, and dancing. In addition, it asked me to dress in either evening or formal attire. There was nothing else on the invitation other than his signature and the date and time he would pick me up.

Curiosity consumed me during my walk. The theater district was home to live bands, the ballet, the opera, and multiple theaters with traveling Broadway shows, performing arts companies, and famous entertainers gracing their stages. Would it be the Alley Theater, Jones Hall, or the mighty Wortham Center? Where would we be going to dinner in our evening attire? Where would we be dancing? What was I going to wear?

Music was always in my family's blood, but the theater was an acquired taste. I took myself and my daughter to intimate concert venues, various operas, and an annual trip to the ballet. Each Christmas it was our tradition to indulge ourselves by purchasing tickets to the classic *Nutcracker*. Our mother-daughter tradition included fine dining, either before or after the ballet, and always involved dressing up. But this invitation was clearly an adults-only date, and I would need to get a sitter.

Over the next four weeks, additional surprises and hints revealing more details about the upcoming evening appeared.

Three weeks away from date night: One morning I found a box of chocolates on my doorstep with a copy of the restaurant menu from where we would be dining. He carefully ensured that the restaurant name was missing from the menu so I still would have no idea where we were heading for dinner when the time came to go on our date. The anticipation was building.

Two weeks away from date night: One evening I came home from work and found a very large red and pink balloon bouquet tied to my front door handle. Wrapped up in the balloon bouquet's tie ribbons was a cassette tape (yes, I am dating myself ... if you don't know what a cassette tape is, Google it). When I popped the tape into my stereo system, I listened to dance music he had recorded from famous classic and pop movies. I got more enthusiastic as I danced in my living room alone, and his gesture once again increased my anticipation of our evening together, now just two weeks away.

The week before date night: I had ended a long day at the office and was walking to my car in the parking lot. As I got closer, I could see something on my windshield. After I emptied the contents of my arms into the back seat, I turned my attention to the package held securely under the wiper blade. It was an unmarked audio CD with a romantic note wrapped around it. I started my car and inserted the CD. It was the soundtrack to the musical *The Phantom of the Opera* by composer and playwright Andrew Lloyd Webber.

For those of you who are not familiar with it, *The Phantom of the Opera* is a romance, mystery, and horror musical based on the 1910 novel written by French author Gaston Leroux. The setting for the novel was the actual Paris opera house, Palais Garnier. The 1896 Helle Opera Act One had just finished when a fire started on the roof of the opera house and melted through a wire holding a counterweight for the chandelier, causing it to fall from the ceiling into the audience, injuring several people and killing one. Leroux used this incident and combined it with tales of a ghost in the opera house to create *Le Fantome de l'Opera*, which was published in 1910 and then translated into English as *The Phantom of the Opera*.

On my drive home, as I continued to listen to the soundtrack, I found it to be foreboding and a bit disturbing. I had not yet seen or read the storyline of this famous classic musical romance, nor would I before our date, as I did not want to create any expectations prior to the show. I wanted to be surprised.

Date Night: The doorbell rang, I opened the front door, and all I could see was an embarrassingly huge bouquet of flowers, so large they concealed the man behind them. I graciously accepted them from his hands, invited him into the entryway, and turned toward the kitchen to locate a few vases so I could place them in water.

Mr. Drama King was extremely disciplined when it came to his fitness regimen, and it paid off like dividends. When I returned to the entryway, he was a sight to behold, with his athletic build making him look like a million bucks in his black tux. Together, we looked like a fairy-tale couple in our formal wear.

I don't remember too much about the restaurant with the exception that I felt overdressed and uncomfortable with the unwanted attention. When we arrived at the theater, there were other operagoers wearing formal evening attire, and we blended in with the crowd easily.

71

Opera is a dramatic story told through song, and this one did not disappoint. It included an opera house ghost, The Phantom, who draws a young maiden he is obsessed with into the dark lair beneath the opera house so he can teach her to sing—so she can sing *his* music. The young maiden falls into his trance, and when she wakes up, she gets a glimpse of him behind his mask. In Act 1, The Phantom hangs a guy that catches a glance of him backstage with the young maiden, then strangles the leading actor, Don Juan, in Act 2 so he can replace him onstage and be with the young maiden. Then, in the end, The Phantom gives the young maiden the choice of staying with him or watching him kill her true love.

With options like those, what's a girl not to like, right?

When the opera ended, our evening continued. He took me to a late-night venue where decadent desserts and a glass of bubbles or one's favorite booze went hand in hand with the low lighting and intimate table setups. We enjoyed our wandering conversation, and I was ready to call it a night as the clock was getting closer to the time that Cinderella's coach would turn back into a pumpkin. When we walked out of the bar, **Mr. Drama King** pointed to the clear sky above and the full moon casting its rays on the street in front of us as he charmingly invited me to dance with him down the middle of the street.

A fantasy evening of being swept off your feet is a lovely indulgence, magical moments between two people can be treasured, and a fairy-tale experience that ends with dancing down the street under the glow of a romantic moon is enticing to dream about.

Make sure, however, that you are not in a faraway trance, causing you to think he is Mr. Right when he might be Mr. Right Now. The impassioned, dramatic, or grand gestures could cause you to be "love-blind" from seeing what else might be in front of you.

Several weeks later, **Mr. Drama King** and I joined a few of my girlfriends at a casual theater event. When the show was over, we stayed out in the courtyard chatting about the storyline. The next thing I knew, he was down on one knee with a ring box in his hand—proposing to me as my friends witnessed the grand gesture unfold. As you can imagine, I was completely caught off guard and struggled to find my bearings. While I appreciated his outgoing nature, his ability to plan, his love of the performing arts, and his desire to create a fantasy, it was very overwhelming, and I had to *walk away* from this proposal.

When a new romantic partner comes into your life and they expend excessive attention on you, showering you with gifts and drowning you in flattery, it can become all-consuming. Some people have termed this kind of behavior at the beginning of a relationship "love bombing," which is creating or manipulating the environment to make it look like they are the perfect mate. Be careful and take a closer look before you leap—being swept off your feet could contribute to you being off-balance, and you might miss the red flags.

The beauty of intentional dating is that it allows you to be in a place of learning more about yourself, your likes, and your preferences as to the types of men you are attracting, enjoying, or not that crazy about. Be grateful for dating, as it's a girl's best friend in the "Is he Mr. Right?" clarifying process.

Sometimes during the dating process, we can create drama in our own lives as things get "louder" because we did not heed the red flag warning signs early in the dating relationship. This can be especially true when we jump from one relationship right into another, which brings me to **Mr. Rebound.**

I was still in my first year of being single again, finding my footing, establishing my routine as a single mother, working full-time, and attempting to get back to being myself in my spare time. This involved examining and shedding religious beliefs that were not mine, exploring the parts of my upbringing that no longer worked and needed to be let go of, considering what I wanted and needed for my daughter and myself, and reclaiming and recreating myself as a healthy person.

When I was newly divorced, I falsely believed that no one would want to date me because I was a divorcee with a toddler. But I was proven wrong in no time. One night I went out with my sister, and **Mr. Rebound** asked me to dance—and yes, he had that perfect combination of dark hair and blue eyes I've always been attracted to.

As we got to know each other over the next several months, I became more aware of his intelligence, his healthy ambition, and his ability to leave work at work. He was just as interested in his life outside of work as he was in his career. He enjoyed golfing and was a family man at heart. He taught me how to play golf, and relax, and he helped me invite fun back into my life.

Mr. Rebound came from what appeared on the outside to be a stable and loving family. His mother and father kept traditional marriage roles based upon gender, with his dad being more dominant in leadership and decision making, along with being the breadwinner, while his mother stayed at home and took care of raising their family and managed the household chores. He had moved to Southern California for business and lived a thousand miles and a full twenty-four-hour drive from his home. He was a family man and really wanted a family of his own.

You never forget your first *real* vacation, and I still remember mine vividly. **Mr. Rebound** took me on my first trip out of the continental United States to Hawaii. It was the first vacation I experienced without other family members or friends. I was grateful that my daughter's father and I had a solid co-parenting relationship and that he had our daughter for the week, which allowed me to take a vacation.

During this time in my life, even though I was not married, I was still heavily engaged in caretaking activities. The sense of over-responsibility I inherited from my mother was in hyper gear. I was a single parent with a toddler, working a full-time job with accountability for my department, and another family member was living with me. In addition, my father had fallen on hard times, needed a place to live, and was asking to borrow money.

I felt so guilt-ridden about going on vacation to Hawaii that I got sick with pneumonia and almost canceled on **Mr. Rebound**. I felt extremely responsible for taking care of my family. It was my mother who said it was "okay" for me to enjoy my life; she encouraged me to go on that vacation and not let feelings of guilt keep me tethered to family members who could take care of themselves.

When **Mr. Rebound** and I landed, we were greeted with wonderful Hawaiian hospitality, including a lei and mai tai punch. I experienced my first pig roast and was mesmerized by the fire dancers at a luau. We enjoyed soaking up the sun, snorkeling on the beautiful beaches, and seriously relaxing.

When I returned from vacation, I went back to work with renewed creativity. I was also assigned to a new division of the company, as they had signed a new contract and were entering the medical waste business. This brought me opportunities to automate the accounting and payroll departments in addition to this new service line. All the work I did was new for the company and soon gained the attention of the corporate headquarters. The chief financial officer (CFO) reached out to me on several occasions to ask if I would consider moving to Texas and join a team being created for the purpose of automating the entire organization's financial systems.

Not knowing that Texans believe everything is bigger and better in their state, I continually gave that CFO a hard time, saying, "You do know I live in Southern California, right? Why would I want to move to Texas?" I had no idea that I might have been coming across as arrogant and potentially offending him. It got to the point that I could no longer ignore his calls, so I took a chance, threw out a dollar figure as my salary request, and he said, "Perfect!" without so much as a little negotiation. I worked things out with my daughter's father, and she and I moved to Houston.

Mr. Rebound and I kept up our long-distance relationship until he decided to interview in the Houston area, and then he made his move to the Lone Star State, where he rented his own apartment. Previously we had dated when my daughter was spending weekends with her father. But now that we lived in the same city, that dynamic changed, and we were now able to spend more than weekend time together, including time with my daughter.

The three of us enjoyed family-type outings at the petting zoo, the neighborhood playground swings, or splashing in the shallow end of a pool. He really loved my daughter as if she were his own, and he wanted us to become his family, but my daughter and I were already a family, and I was looking for a partner.

One evening, after we both had a full day at our jobs, he was sitting in my living room while I was taking care of my daughter's evening activities and cooking dinner. I could feel myself getting more upset by the minute that he was sitting and relaxing in front of the television while I was running around.

He could clearly see that I was upset, and he had the emotional maturity to ask what I was upset about. I told him I was upset because he was watching television while I was cooking his dinner. In a very calm voice, he got my attention when he said, **"I didn't ask you to cook my dinner."**

His answer astounded me, and it stopped me right in my tracks. I stood in the middle of the living room, stunned. Oh my God! He was so right! He never once asked me to cook his dinner. I was unconsciously repeating the same role my mother performed when we were kids. I was still playing the conventional wife role exemplified and praised in the church and in our society. We weren't even married, yet I still assumed the traditional marriage gender role of being a nurturer and homemaker, and I believed that he expected me to cook his dinner. It never crossed my mind to ask him if he wanted or expected me to cook for him, and in the moment of his illuminating comment, I realized that I was still *hostage to my own robotic thinking.*

How could I untangle myself from my unconscious habits?

How could I be a healthier me, so I could bring a more conscious version of myself into a relationship?

Bottom line: I still did not know myself, nor had I taken significant time in between relationships to become more self-aware. I needed more time to be with myself or I could risk recreating the same unfulfilling experiences I had unconsciously created in the past.

I was grateful that **Mr. Rebound** lived in his own apartment on the other side of the city because I naively believed that it would make it easier for me to create more space between us. He really wanted to be married and have a family with my daughter and me. I knew that I was not anywhere near being ready for marriage again. We kept dating, although infrequently, knowing that we both wanted different things—neither one of us honestly acknowledging the reality of our misaligned directions.

A few months had gone by since we had seen each other, and he was involved in a late-night automobile accident. The golf clubs in the back of his vehicle were not secured and flew to the front of the car, hitting him and causing serious lacerations to his face and head. He called me the next day when they released him from the emergency room and asked me to come pick him up.

When I arrived at the hospital to get him, I could visibly see the stitches, the matted blood in multiple locations on his head, and dried blood stains on his arms, face, and clothing. It was evident that he was in no condition to care for himself. Once we were back at his apartment, I got him out of his throwaway shirt, and I warmed up a basin of soapy water. I gently cleaned the blood off him and then softly washed his hair until all the blood was gone and only the stitches remained. While he rested, I went to the store to purchase food that would be easy for him to eat and prepare for himself during his healing process.

It took a while for his body to heal and the body of his car to be fixed. Once he was back to himself, he called me and asked if he could come over to my house. I didn't want us to continue dating and told him I didn't think it was a good idea. Then he asked if we could just meet somewhere in the middle and talk. Again, I told him I didn't think it was a good idea since it would just make it harder for us to move forward with our own lives. He pressed further and asked if we could meet just one more time and talk things out.

I gave in, against my better judgment, and agreed to meet in the middle. He picked a hotel parking lot right off the busy freeway that connected one side of the city to the other. I arrived first. I parked my car, got out of it, and leaned against the car door on the driver's side. He arrived, joined me, and then asked if we could go into the hotel lobby to talk. I didn't fall for that and told him anything we had to say to each other could be said right where we were.

As we began to talk, we heard car tires squealing as they turned and screeched to a halt in the hotel parking lot. We instinctively turned our heads in their direction as cars pulled into every driveway, blocking any cars from getting out. We then watched a crime scene unfold as the flood of unmarked cars opened their doors and the shouting and shooting began.

At the first sound of gunfire, I immediately dropped down on my knees to curl up next to my tire in between my car and the one beside it. **Mr. Rebound** was still standing in shock, so I reached up and pulled him down to the ground with me. Once the gunfire halted, we could hear law enforcement agents calling to one another that it was all clear.

When we felt it was safe to stand up, we got to our feet. Our view was filled with unmarked cars, people in FBI jackets, and plainclothes people wearing flak jackets. Two cars were being searched for drugs and weapons, and several individuals were face down on the parking lot pavement with their hands cuffed behind their backs.

With every exit blocked, we weren't going anywhere, and no doubt with us being at the scene of the crime, they would be coming to question us shortly.

Standing in the hotel parking lot, in disbelief at everything that just unfolded, I told **Mr. Rebound** that this was a sign we should both pay attention to—that we should walk fast—no, run—and not see each other anymore before something worse happened to us both. I am grateful that he did not pursue it any longer as I was resolved to not have this level of dangerous drama in my and my daughter's lives. Too much drama could be a sign that someone hungers for attention; seldom does drama occur in healthy relationships, and that is exactly what I wanted in my life.

Introspection Questions

1. Have you ever wished someone would sweep you off your feet?
2. Why would you like to have the experience of being swept off your feet?
3. What experiences from romance novels or Hallmark movies would you like to see take place in real life for you? What would those experiences provide for you? Can you give those experiences to yourself?
4. Spend some time reflecting on your past relationships. Did your partner make any grand gestures? Reflect on the feeling you had when he made those grand gestures. Were his grand gestures really just for you, for him, or for others?
5. Did you ever wish a man would make grand gestures? If so, why? What would those grand gestures provide or say to you? What might your interpretation be?
6. Looking at your past or current relationship, where did your partner sweep you off your feet, leaving you potentially off balance?
7. Looking at your past relationships, where might you have been dreamy or in a trance about him, leaving you love-blind? What did you not see? What can you clearly see now? If you are currently in a relationship, are those same things visible now?
8. Does your partner believe that he must sweep you off your feet?
9. What conversations could you two have about your relationship based in reality versus a fairy tale?
10. Make a list of all your relationships and review them to consider:
    a. "Things" that might have been moving too fast. What was moving too fast for you, potentially keeping you off balance and unable to see more of what was in front of you?
    b. Was the relationship a repeat of something familiar? What was familiar? What continues to repeat itself? Do you want it to repeat? If not, why do you keep attracting it?

11. What was significant in your family upbringing? What were the things your mom or dad or significant caretaker did in the family, for you and for the family? What are (or were) your expectations or wants from your husband/significant other/ partner? Are these roles traditional or nontraditional?

12. How much did you know/do you know about your partner's family upbringing? What were the things his mom or dad or significant caretaker did in the family—specifically, for him? What were his father's expectations of his wife? Are these roles traditional or nontraditional?

13. What did you not do for yourself, or put off doing for yourself, in your past relationships? Why? What got in the way? Was your partner supportive of what you wanted? How did he show that support?

14. What are you *not* doing for yourself in your current relationship? Self-care? Travel? Spending time with your friends? Exercising? What keeps you from doing it?

15. What have you felt responsible for or obligated to do in past relationships that didn't feel good? What about in current relationships?

16. What was your partner responsible for or obligated to do in your past relationship that didn't feel good? What about in your current relationship?

17. What is your definition of a vacation? How do you like to travel?

18. What is your partner's definition of a vacation? How does he like to travel?

19. What things do you automatically assume you need to do in the relationship?

20. Where have you recreated the same unfulfilling relationship experiences?

21. What are the things you do in relationships that you have always done?

22. Whether in dating or traveling or in longer-term relationships, what roles do you find yourself playing that resemble those

of your parents? Your ethnic or religious culture? Are they truly you or have they become an unconscious expression that could use further examination?

23. What does "he do" or what did "he do" that has upset you in past or current relationships? What did you naturally assume about his actions? What did you determine was the root cause of his actions? If he were standing in front of you now, what questions could you ask him so he could reveal to you what he was thinking?

24. What drama, actions, or activities are the same or familiar in your current relationship or across past relationships?

25. What behaviors do you automatically assume (traditional/non-traditional/conventional) because you believe you are supposed to be "that way" in a relationship? If you made a list, would you be able to have an honest dialogue with someone else to see if they still work for you, him, and the relationship?

26. Where might you be shaping, changing, or molding yourself to fit someone else's beliefs? Are they truly that other person's beliefs or what you think might be their beliefs?

27. Where might you be a hostage to your own habits or thinking?

28. In what ways can you be a healthier version of yourself? What support can you ask your partner for to ensure that you get what you need to be a healthier version of yourself?

29. What do you do with your time in between relationships?

30. What relationships were already over that you allowed to linger longer than was healthy for you or them?

31. What are your red flags or signs that the relationship is over?

32. Did you ever ignore the red flags or signs and wished you had not? How long did you ignore them? What was your moment-of-truth attention getter?

33. What did it cost you or your family because you stepped over the warnings?

34. What stopped you from ending the relationship sooner?

CHAPTER 7

SEMICONSCIOUS (STEPPING OVER SIGNS)

It was **Mr. Childlike's** birthday, and I planned his celebration at Dave & Buster's® Sports Bar, an epic center of shiny objects and entertainment. He loved everything about the party place including the multitude of wide-screen televisions  adorning every wall, their extensive menu of craft beers, cocktails, and food, and the hundreds of arcade and video games begging to be played so you can rack up points and convert them into carnival-like prizes.

As his friends and family arrived, I provided them with a starter string of arcade tickets and pointed them in the direction of the server who would take their drink order. The party was off to a good start, and after an hour of playing arcade games, the guests had worked up an appetite. As they drifted in from the gaming area, they were greeted with a table full of appetizers, sliders, and salads. After the food was ravaged, we moved on to multiple desserts that would satisfy any sweet tooth.

It was all fun and games ... until it wasn't. Many guests had already left, and I stood talking with **Mr. Childlike's** best friend and his wife as they were getting ready to leave when their four-year-old daughter tugged on my shirt and asked me if I was **Mr. Childlike's** mommy. Awkward!

Out of the mouths of babes, the truth was spoken, and I stood there busted ... at Dave & Busters.

His best friend had introduced us a few years earlier. **Mr. Childlike** was the youngest of four and a wickedly smart man with the mindset of an inventor. He was committed to conserving the earth's resources and reducing pollution, especially when it came to what was being dumped in our landfills. He was highly educated in mathematics and the physical sciences and was particularly engaging and gifted at translating those ideas into everyday reality.

We were swimming one warm summer afternoon when he stopped, stood up, and said, "Watch." I can still see him standing in the pool taking both hands and scooping up large double handfuls of water out of the pool, tossing them high into the air just so I could be dazzled by the sun's rays creating prisms of color-filled light through every drop as they cascaded back down into the pool. He did this repeatedly as he explained the science behind refracted light when light is dispersed into seven colors, creating a rainbow effect. I was both impressed and taken by his sense of childlike wonder as he stopped and took the time to delight in the elegance of nature, something scientific, and simply beautiful.

At this point in my life, I had been single for more years than I had been married. I was also advancing my career and engaged in various forms of my own self-reflection and development. I thought that I knew myself better, assumed that I was healthier when it came to relationships, and felt ready to be in a committed relationship again. I was also working toward becoming a more conscious and quicker creator by developing my *intentionality skills*. This is the practice of being deliberate and resolute in your beliefs and desires while directing them toward a specific result or outcome you would like to produce or experience.

I desired to have **Mr. Childlike** propose to me. I wrote down my clear intention on a piece of paper, and *within a week, he proposed*. Surprised by my high-speed results, I too was like a little kid, newly learning how to place my hands on the wheel of creation by creating what I wanted, fueling my goals and desires with my intentions. This is exactly the situation where someone says, "Be careful what you ask for, you just might get it!"

We discussed how we wanted our wedding to take place before the end of the year, and then took turns calling our family and friends and telling them we were engaged. I will never forget the conversation we had when we shared the news with his best friend and attorney. His best friend's response was unceremonious and foretelling when he said, "Congratulations you two, and if you ever get divorced, *I will represent her.*"

Mr. Childlike and I agreed that he would plan and pay for the honeymoon, and I would plan and pay for the wedding and wedding reception. With both of us renting our own places, we added house hunting and moving from two homes into one to the already long list of things to accomplish in a short period of time.

One evening he invited me over to his parents' house. He wasn't quite forthcoming with his reason for the get-together, but that soon unfolded shortly after dinner was over. We moved into the living room, and he became noticeably uncomfortable, shifting his position on the couch as he began to talk, asking his parents for a considerably large sum of money. Then I became uncomfortable. I felt I was being used as a form of protection for him to keep his parents from saying no to his request. Before we left that evening, he had a check in hand.

We located a home and moved into it, including his unrestrained dog and my low-maintenance cat. He previously had a bachelor pad with limited furniture, leaving the vast majority of bedroom, living room, dining room, and décor furnishings in our new home coming from my place. The largest big-screen televisions I had ever seen came from the groom-to-be's place and were now the center of attention in both the living room and our bedroom.

We had a lovely wedding ceremony and a fun party reception with beautiful picture memories. When we went to leave for our honeymoon, he asked me to stop by an ATM machine on our way out of town. I made the ATM stop, and when he got back into the car, he noted that he did not have enough cash, and asked if I could float him funds when he needed them. My heart dropped. I felt that

I had been duped again. Darn it! I lived up to my agreement in the wedding and reception planning and funding. I was disappointed that he would not be living up to his end of the agreement. Hardly a trusting or reliable foundation for starting on our road together.

The Honeymoon's Definitely Over

When we came back from the honeymoon, reality hit harder: The party was over. I went back to work while he worked on his entrepreneurial inventions. I worked in the information technology industry as a business consultant. My job required that I travel every week to my clients' location. This involved flying out every Sunday night and returning every Thursday night. The name for this type of traveling consultant is a "road warrior."

Because I could not leave the client site until after 5:00 p.m., I frequently arrived home late on Thursday nights when he was already asleep on the couch or in our bed with one or both televisions still playing. It was not an ideal way to begin a new marriage with me being on the road each week, always gone five nights out of seven.

Our relationship, just like his dog, did not have the benefit of consistent direction and attention. The dog did whatever she wanted, and it wasn't even a year before my light blue couch and loveseat were blood-stained, tattered, and soiled beyond repair, much like the fabric of our relationship.

Even when I was home, there was no real connection. He wasn't sharing about the progress of his inventions, and when I asked him about his work, I felt that he was evading me with his ambiguous answers. We did not have a common interest to pursue together, nor did we have any shared spiritual beliefs. I found him sleeping or zoned out in front of the television more than he was engaged in his life or ours.

During my sixty-five hours at home each weekend, I was usually restocking the refrigerator, washing our clothes, paying our bills, ensuring the pets got to the vet in addition to coordinating the housekeeping and house maintenance tasks. My experience was parenting not partnering, which was not a workable situation for either of us. It got to the point where I could not wait to get back on that plane and leave my married (parental) life behind. I resented him for putting me in a position to be the parent while he acted like an irresponsible teenager.

Within six weeks of being outed by a child at Dave & Busters for my motherly aura and parental persona, I was once again reminded that I still was not healthy enough to be in a committed relationship. I easily fell back into the habit of being over-responsible for things that I did not need to take on. I was part of the problem, creating a mother/child-type relationship, stepping in and taking care of things that he could take care of himself.

I found myself crying more than I was happy. Plus, I knew from my coaching experiences that you get the relationship and relationship experiences that you tolerate.

What was I thinking?

What was I **not** being mindful of that produced the unwanted results I was experiencing in this relationship? What did I not see while we were dating? Why did I not see it? What else was I still love-blind to?

Then one Saturday morning, an extraordinary thing happened. I was taking a shower when I heard a very distinctive voice ask, "Are you moving out before your birthday or after?" The voice was not asking *if* I was going to move out. The voice was asking *when* I was going to move out. This voice left an unforgettable impression.

As synchronicity would have it, I also had a tarot card reading scheduled for noon on this same day with a woman highly regarded for her expert psychic and mediumship abilities. I had not met with her before and I had no idea what other skills she might integrate into the card reading, as readers have all kinds of backgrounds and may incorporate astrology, numerology, or the Kabbalah's Jewish mysticism.

The tarot tells stories about our life segments—the segments of life that are our present, past, potential future, and current challenges, including ourselves and the people in our lives. After I shuffled the tarot card deck, I handed it back to her and she laid out ten cards in the traditional Celtic Cross format. What really stood out for me was the Tower card and its significance. As I stared at the Tower card, upright and in my face, I could see that the Tower had been struck by lightning, flames were pouring out of each window, and the king and queen had lept out of the Tower and were falling to their deaths on the ground below.

The card reader shared the multiple interpretations of this card, denoting that it represented destruction or failure, intense and sudden change, higher learning and liberation, a spectacular ambition that ends in disaster, death or divorce, and the possibility of a fresh start. The information associated with this card coupled with the voice I heard less than two hours earlier provided me with an unexpected moment of pure clarity. Was I going to stay in this relationship of sorrow or was I going to choose joy? It was so uncomplicated. Was I going to choose sorrow or joy? It was very straightforward. It was so simple: joy or sorrow. Choose! What was it going to be for me?

This new insight and thinking was liberating. Without any delay, I changed my intentions to choosing joy! In the blink of an eye, a whole new canvas opened up in front of me. I started talking about the possibility of packing my things, placing them in storage, and moving in with one of my girlfriends. Then the card reader with psychic abilities said, "But you don't even like this state!" She was so right, but how did she know that? I hated the heat, poor air quality, scorpions, and snakes. Instantaneously, another new possibility opened: I could live *anywhere*.

Like every other Sunday night, I flew out of the state and back to my customer's location. As divine providence would have it, the vice president of our division was going to be joining our team for the upcoming week's activities. Working for this company was amazing. They didn't just give lip service to the rhetoric most companies espouse surrounding the way they value their employees. The company honestly believed that if they took care of their employees, the employees would take care of their customers. Then they put their money where their mouth was by paying us quarterly bonuses based upon the profits we generated in our respective units. When you work for a company you love, and you are blessed to work on a high-performance team that is committed to one another professionally and personally, it is a thing of beauty.

We were a tight-knit team and cared about one another. This project had huge visibility across the company and would be going on for at least a year. During the week, I spoke with my boss about the personal life changes I was considering, and he replied, "If anyone deserves to be happy, it's you." Then he backed up those words by stating that the company would hire someone to pack my things and move them to the city in which we were working so I could focus on the job at hand. In addition, they would locate a few apartments for me to consider. This was a serious win/win solution that I never dreamed would happen. It saved the customer and my company travel-related expenses for a year. They made my transition effortless and allowed me to remove the strain of traveling from my life. My husband's best friend represented both of us and filed the divorce papers free of charge with the court system. I woke up on my birthday in my new apartment, in a new state, alone and happy with a fresh start.

When your soul wants you to go in a different direction, it will stop at nothing to reorganize your life. **Mr. Childlike** was a unique soul mate on my love story journey. In under just two years' time, he caused my soul to grow tremendously.

1. I was able to put my hands on the wheel of creation by getting him to propose to me. I also realized that I semiconsciously created him to propose to me when I had not fully clarified all that I wanted to create in the first place. The most important revelation was learning that I could undo my creation just as quickly as I manifested it.
2. **Mr. Childlike** reintroduced fun, wonder, and curiosity into my life.

3. **Mr. Childlike** taught me that I need to get much more curious about the men I date and ask way more questions. What a gift!

The Love Lab

In 2005, years after my second divorce, Malcolm Gladwell's book *Blink* was released. Throughout the book, he points out the ways in which first impressions help us make the right decision in some situations and may deceive us in others. It was a fascinating read about understanding the human mind and decision-making, exposing me to cutting-edge use cases from the fields of neuroscience and psychology.

One of the use cases involved Dr. John Gottman and Dr. Robert Levenson's Love Lab. Since the 1970s, with his background in mathematics, statistics, and psychology, Dr. John Gottman had been using science and data to see if he could firmly link actual relationship interactional patterns to marital happiness or divorce outcomes. I was fascinated by the application of clinical research toward discovering how couples create and maintain friendship and intimacy and their relationship to conflict.

After forty years of research with thousands of couples, Dr. John Gottman has authored more than two hundred published academic articles, authored, or co-authored more than forty books, and is known for his work on marital stability and his more than 90 percent accuracy surrounding the prediction of couples headed for divorce. Dr. Julie Gottman, clinical psychologist and researcher, along with her husband, Dr. John Gottman, are co-founders of the Gottman Institute, and they leveraged the original couples laboratory and reimagined it for the twenty-first century. The physical Love Lab is in Seattle, Washington, where they use state-of-the-art physiological monitoring equipment and an emotional observation system that supports their research-based approach to relationships.

The institute continues to evolve in its commitment for couples to have the data surrounding their relationships strengths and challenge areas. It provides its "Art and Science of Love" workshop attendees with evidence-based information, coaching, and materials enabling them to keep their relationship moving in a positive direction. They have created a well-being platform with multiple services, including leveraging machine learning and artificial intelligence in their virtual Love Lab for couples at Gottman.com.

Your intuition, heart, and body will provide you with lots of information on whether he is Mr. Right or Mr. Right Now. When it comes to matters of the heart, balancing your head and heart might be better achieved by obtaining additional data surrounding your couple strengths and challenge areas. Enabled with data, you can ask additional questions that support you both in more consciously creating your love story.

Shoulda, Coulda, Woulda

Hindsight can be 20/20 if you are willing to see the reality of your situation from several angles. It might be even more advantageous to see you, your partner, and your relationship from all the angles provided by the Love Lab before you get engaged or married. I did not have the benefit of this research when I was dating or even during my first two marriages. However, there were multiple discussions that I stepped over without engaging in a conversation with **Mr. Childlike.** Without the benefit of machine learning or artificial intelligence, I bet you caught many of them:

1. I had been married before and he was a bachelor; we naturally would have different perspectives.
2. I was the second of four in my family order and he was the baby in his; we grew up with different levels of family engagement.
3. We had different versions of what a home should look like, and creating one together is much more than the act of combining furniture.
4. Even though we both loved dogs and cats, the lack of pet management became a source of perceived disrespect.

5. When his best friend stated that if we ever got divorced, he would represent me, I neglected to follow up that comment with, "What do you know that I am not aware of? What do you see that I don't?"
6. I was gone almost five days a week. What were his needs while I was away and what were my needs when I was at home?
7. How was he earning his money? Why did he feel the need to ask his parents for money? Why did he spring that conversation on me in front of them?
8. What were his inventions? What was the market for those inventions and who was going to purchase them?
9. Why could he not keep his word when it came to our honeymoon? What happened?
10. If I wanted a real partnership, then why was I still interacting with my husband like a parent and not a partner? I was still bringing my parenting persona to relationships versus a partnership or adult persona. My parenting persona would continue to attract the type of men who are not partnership material.

Had I not ignored the signs and spent more time asking questions, I would have learned enough to know that he was not my Mr. Right, and he would have been a Mr. Right Now. That would have saved us both from the cost of getting married and the pain surrounding divorce. From my experienced perspective, I should have been planning for the foundation of our marriage and partnership *with him*, instead of planning a wedding and reception on my own.

Worldpopulationreview.com notes that about 50 percent of married couples divorce, giving the United States the sixth highest divorce rate in the world.

At the Whitley Law Firm,[15] they point to numerous studies noting that nearly 70 percent of divorces are initiated by women, and among college-educated women, this number jumps to 90 percent.

---

[15] WhitleyLawFirmPC.com.

The main driving factors include household inequality, women taking on more of the emotional burden for the entire household, and women no longer tolerating consistent unacceptable behavior.

Legaljob.io notes there are over 750,000 divorces in the U.S. each year and as noted above, nearly 70 percent of those divorces are initiated by the wife. Studies suggest that out of most marriages that fail, roughly 10 percent will do so within the first two years and 60 percent of all divorces involve individuals in the age range of twenty-five to thirty-nine.

Looks like I may not be the only one who planned a wedding when I should have been spending more time learning about who I was about to get in bed with. Another opportunity to grow and more consciously create my love story.

Introspection Questions

1. Have you or a friend ever spent more time planning the wedding instead of planning the partnership?
2. Are you both able to be honest with full disclosure by showing each other the money? What money conversations need to be explored surrounding each person's employment income, benefits, savings, investments, sole proprietor income, contractual agreements, business partnership income and liabilities, retirement savings and investment income, family or potential for inheritance income, prenuptial agreements, named beneficiaries, trust funds, land and property holdings, tax return filings, and IRS taxes due? What do you each think about and believe about money? How did your/their family teach you/them to handle money? Do you/they know how to budget, live within a budget, or read a bank statement? Is everything that you/he plan to bring into the relationship protected and respected?
3. How do you approach working and earning money? How do you feel or think you would feel should you make more income than he does or less income than he does? How does

93

he approach working and earning money? How does he feel or think he would feel if you made more income or less income than him?

4. Do you give your word and keep it? Do you do what you say you are going to do and then do it? On time? When you might go over the time you promised, do you communicate that to your boyfriend or fiancé? Will he make commitments? Does he do what he says he will do in the time he said he would do it?

5. Where does each of you fall in the family order? Were you born the youngest and he the oldest? Are you both only children? What family dynamic was created for each of you based on your birth order? Are you both consciously aware of the potential for the same dynamics in your marriage relationship? How will you support each other in moving beyond those old family patterns in order to create what works better for the two of you?

6. What are the family and friend dynamics? Do your friends like him? What do your closest friends and family have to say about him? Do they include him and enjoy spending time with him, or do they avoid him? Have you given up your friends to spend more time with him? Do his friends and family like you? Do they include you?

7. When it comes to health, what are your thoughts about fitness and what condition are you/he in? How is your/his mental and physical health? What is your/his ideas for and needs surrounding nutrition? What medications are you/he on? How do you/he exercise individually and/or together?

8. What are your goals, aspirations, and vision for your life? What are his goals, aspirations, and vision for his life? Where and how do you plan to support each other in reaching those goals, aspirations, and visions of being and experiencing your best versions of yourselves? Where are you aligned in those goals and aspirations? Where do feel supported or not feel supported by him? Where does he feel supported or not feel supported by you?

9. What are you stepping over? What are you tolerating or putting up with? What are you not addressing or avoiding as a topic of discussion? Can you find a way to talk about these sensitive topics without pointing fingers or being aggressive?

10. Do either of you want children or do not want children? If you do want children, how many and by when? If you do want children, do either of you expect the other to carry out traditional parenting roles or give up their jobs? If yes, what are the roles to be played by each parent, and for how long before the other parent can return to the workforce, should you choose together?

CHAPTER 8

BRIEF, BRILLIANT, AND GONE

There are 3.97 billion men in the world representing 50.42 percent of the total population.[16]

- Who told you there could only be one Prince Charming or one soul mate for you?
- Where did you hear that you even needed to have a Prince Charming or soul mate?
- Where did you learn marriage was a requirement or an expectation or perhaps the Holy Grail for relationships?
- What was the source of that data?
- Where did you learn that piece of information?
- How early did this idea get placed in your thinking?
- When did you come to think or believe there could only be one?

Let's do the math.

This belief dictates that there is one Prince Charming or one soul mate to be found out of almost 3.97 billion potential candidates.

---

[16] https://m.staticticstimes.com.

This belief also drives us to push or even force the form of our relationships into a marriage or committed state.

There is this idea that there is only one person out there for each of us who can make us whole and happy.

Perhaps you were told since you were little that one day you will find the one? There is a constant barrage of "waiting for your Prince Charming" or "searching for your soul mate" information being propagated by The Walt Disney Company, magazines, fairy tales, family members, philosophers, books, television shows, media, and movies, leaving us waiting for Jerry Maguire to get his act together, come to his senses, and say, "You complete me."

Perhaps it is time to challenge this thinking.

We are not the broken half, looking for the other half so we can feel whole. We don't need someone else to do or be that for us. We are whole and complete on our own. The women I know are off-the-hook amazing, embodying a multitude of talents, including an enormous capacity to love with unequaled resiliency. Women have stereotypically been portrayed as sex objects, mothers, the other woman, wives, suffering, weak, or submissive. This perpetuates down to our children and grandchildren and it's not at all a complete representation of who we are as women.

As of the writing of this book, I have appreciated dating different men for more than twenty years over the course of my life. I have experienced extreme value in dating. Dating all different kinds of men has allowed me to better clarify what my preferences in men are and are not. It has allowed me to better determine the type of relationship with men I wanted and did not want.

Dating allowed me to gain greater clarity surrounding my own wants and needs. Dating allowed me to practice asking for what I wanted, practice and improve my ability to speak up when my opinions were different from his, and practice being open, honest, and asking for what I wanted in my communications when it was vulnerable to do so.

My dating was in no way one-sided. The men I dated were also in a similar position. They could choose to explore dating in the same manner, or not.

Widening the Playing Field

If you were to walk in my teenage room, you would have seen picture after picture of me with a different guy at every high school dance function. Whether you were looking at the annual Sadie Hawkins, Homecoming Dance, or my prom pictures, each one had a different guy standing next to me. Scott, Tim, Doug, Gordy, Dan, and so on, all handsomely displayed on my bedroom shelves. During my early dating years, I dated guys from my school, other schools, guys I worked with, and guys I met at social functions.

Occasionally, I would date a few at the same time.

I remember one day hearing the phone ring and as I went downstairs to answer it, my mother reached the phone before I did. I just cringed as she asked the guy on the other end of the phone, "Is this Danny?" I could hear the guy on the other end of the phone say it was not. Then my mother handed me the phone to deal with the cleanup.

After getting off that phone call, I went into the kitchen and had a little meeting with my sister and mother to provide them with specific instructions on how to take calls for me. The conversation with the two of them went like this:

"When someone calls for me, just say, 'May I ask who is calling?'" I asked them not to guess their names or presume they knew who it was as I did not want them to blow my cover.

My mother responded, "I think that I do pretty good considering you change boyfriends like you change clothes." Her comments did not slow me down one bit.

If you are a teenager or in your twenties, you are exposed to so many new things. Perhaps these years, ages fourteen through twenty-nine, are for figuring out what you like and what you don't like. Perhaps these years are for you to explore different adventures so you can select the direction you would your life to take. This could be the best time for you to identify all the things you would like to experience during your lifetime so you have more information, enabling you to better determine if you want to get married or be in a committed relationship.

Unconscious influences quite often drive us to "couple." Whether it comes from religious texts, cultural norms, governmental incentives, Hallmark movies, romance novels, or Disney fairy tales, we are programmed to narrow the playing field to exclusively date one person, be in a committed relationship, become engaged, or get married.

So how do you not let "coupling" run the show? How can you open the playing field so you can explore your preferences and learn more about yourself, what you want, and grow?

The first thing is just to become aware of the unconscious influences that might drive you to choose a Mr. Right when he should be a Mr. Right Now. The awareness of your unconscious influences alone will bring more consciousness to your dating activities. You will recognize when you or the person you're dating is trying to drive the relationship into a particular direction, pushing for exclusivity in some form when it might be best to linger and further explore the relationship over a longer period.

Times Are Changing

In the 1950s women felt tremendous pressure to get a wedding ring because marriage and children were the national agenda. The United States was pushing domesticity and the nuclear family as superior to the Russian way of life. Women were encouraged to get their M.R.S. degree in college by finding a man and becoming his Mrs. Now, here we are seventy years later, and the percentage of the U.S. population who have completed college by gender is 36.7 percent male versus 38.3 percent female, as reported by Statista. com.

Once upon a time in America, marriage was the norm for adults. But now, for the first time since the Bureau of Labor Statistics began tracking these numbers in 1976, there are more single Americans than people who are married. That is a huge change. About

50.2 percent—or 124.6 million American adults—are single. In 1950, that number was about 22 percent.

With all the dating sites and meetup applications available with one touch on our smartphones, it is easier to meet people from around the world than those next door with a few clicks. Even though it is easier to meet people, people today are more selective and not willing to compromise.

How can you widen your dating playing field? How can you learn about your own preferences and desires along the way, gaining clarity and building your internal foundation without taking decades to figure it out like me? Perhaps we can learn to have some fun, change the conversation, and take the stress out of dating. Here is one way to expand your perspective and think about it from another vantage point.

A Buffet of Men, over 3.97 Billion to Be Exact

When you go to a buffet, do you only taste one food?

How do you know which foods you will enjoy or not enjoy on the buffet?

That's right. You pick up a dish. You survey your choices by walking around to see everything that the buffet has to offer. You ask yourself, *What do I really want?* You put a little bit of a few enticing things on your plate and then go back to your table. You take silverware in hand and taste them one by one, savoring each item. You may even take the time to notice the texture, smell the aroma, or gauge the layers of seasonings used.

How can you possibly know who Mr. Right is when you haven't dated the Mr. Right Nows? How can you be so sure that he is Mr. Right when you don't have any or much experience engaging with men?

What if you approached dating like you do a buffet? It could be a fun and lighthearted perspective for exploring your options and getting the most out of your dating experience.

Dos and Don'ts of Eating at a Buffet	Dos and Don'ts of Exploring the Buffet of Men
Do eat a snack before going to the buffet. Being too hungry can lead you to eat too quickly and overindulge the same way that you would not go to the supermarket on an empty stomach to avoid overspending.	**Do satisfy yourself.** How can you satisfy yourself by taking care of your needs, practicing self-compassion or self-care first before jumping on those dating apps or going out on a date so you don't dive into the deep end on the first, second, or third date?
Do browse. Look at all the selections before eating. Don't choose the first thing that looks appetizing. Instead, take a walk around the entire buffet, taking note of what is being offered and looks good to you. Exploring the contents of the buffet will also help you avoid eating food that you don't really like or eating too much.	**Do explore your preferences.** This can be accomplished both virtually and physically. As you scroll through the dating app profiles, keep notes on the things you like and don't like or find intriguing or deal breakers in the men's profiles you review. Take yourself out or go out with a girlfriend and couple watch. Notice how the various couples treat or engage with each other. Take notes on how you want or don't want your relationship to take form or express itself.
Do consider an appetizer-sized plate and choose smaller portions or start off with lighter foods. It is tempting to take larger portions of something that looks delicious but avoid this. Going back for seconds or thirds is perfectly acceptable. So that you leave room in your stomach, start with an appetizer before diving into heavier foods.	**Do micro-date.** Test-drive your preferences with an ice cream, coffee, or walk in the park date. Keep it brief. As you date men in small portions, remember to go back to your preferences list and update it with your new possibilities. Further clarify, in writing, the things you like and don't like as you learn more about yourself and your preferences.
Do pick foods you would not cook for yourself or expand your palate tasting gourmet foods. Buffets can offer many delicious familiar foods and while these are tasty, look for things that you would not cook for yourself and try new foods, so the experience becomes a treat.	**Do "not your type."** Ever wonder why you keep hitting the repeat button and attracting the same relationships? Dating the same type can be limiting. Expand your man palate by taking a chance on several different men. You just may surprise yourself!

BRIEF, BRILLIANT, AND GONE

Dos and Don'ts of Eating at a Buffet	Dos and Don'ts of Exploring the Buffet of Men
Do be cautious and aware. Consider how long the food has been sitting out. Look to see if you are in a cheap buffet where you might end up being disappointed. When you come across something you do not truly enjoy, stop eating, leave it on the plate and choose something else. If it is difficult to know how long the food has been sitting out, you may need to ASK.	**Don't talk about your exes, past relationships, marriages, or children.** Think about good early-dating questions you want to ask so you can truly get to know the character of the human being you are meeting. Discover how they are similar or different from you. Do they exhibit healthy character traits like respect and forgiveness or unhealthy character traits like criticism or distrust? See if you like the human being you are with so you can decide if you want to spend time on a second date.
Do enjoy yourself, pace yourself, and eat slowly. You will only get your money's worth if each bite you take is worth something for you. Enjoy that food. If you eat too fast, it can make you feel too full, and you will not be able to enjoy as much as you initially wanted if you would have paced yourself. Chew slowly as you eat and take breaths between bites. Wait a minute or two before going back for seconds.	**Do enjoy yourself and delight in developing your ability to be in a relationship with another person.** Dating is a great opportunity to practice self-compassion, as you will not always get it right. Even if you grew up with healthy relationship examples, they are not hereditary and do not get passed down from generation to generation. There is no guarantee that you know how to do this. See how long you can enjoy the dating process and your experiences. Avoid figuring out if he is father or marriage material. Avoid forcing the relationship into a specific form (exclusive, committed, or marriage). Trust the process of simply getting to know each other. Is the person a match for you energetically and emotionally?

Brief, Brilliant, and Gone Guys

Because I lived in various cities, I dated quite a bit on Match.com. It was always interesting to see who I would meet and what new adventures I could enjoy with another person. I was not ready to settle down, nor was I sure about my interest in getting married again. Knowing those two things about myself and being able to date free from concern about the form the relationship would take enabled me to have more freedom in my communications and allowed me to practice speaking honestly with love and respect.

After you have opened the dating playing field and you are exploring different types of men, how do you know when to move on? Here are three examples of what I call brief, brilliant, and gone dating relationships:

Mr. Mom was a sales engineer and a serious cyclist. He had little to no body fat and was deep into interval training. He had an amicable divorce, two adorable little girls he had every other weekend for at least forty-eight hours, and spoke positively about his former wife.

For the first few months we dated, we met at mutually agreed-upon locations during the weekends the children were with their mother. Then one Saturday, he invited me to his home when the children were with him.

It did not take long for me to see that **Mr. Mom** was in his infancy at being a full-time parent. Even though he retained their original home, there was absolutely no order or organization to be found. The cupboards were in disarray, with dishes, Tupperware, and pots and pans stuffed anywhere and everywhere. There was food in the refrigerator and prescription meds in the spice cabinets with long-overdue expiration dates.

Mr. Mom also had no idea how to play or just be with his daughters. The television set ran endlessly to keep them occupied and toys covered the floors in most rooms throughout the house. When I began to play with them, it wasn't long before I noticed he had disappeared into his fitness room and could be found on his workout bike.

Brief – I got curious and asked more questions about his needs. It became clear to me that he was not looking for a relationship for himself, he was looking for a part-time mother for his daughters and someone to handle his household.

Brilliant – What I learned about myself. There was a time in my life when this scenario would have played on my need to be needed and I would have stepped in and parented two children that already had two capable parents. The truth of the situation became clearer as we talked. He was newly divorced, and this was a growth opportunity for him to learn to engage with his daughters. I had already raised my daughter and this dating experience enabled me to think more clearly about what I wanted in a future partner. I updated my relationship preferences list, noting that I preferred to date men with no children or date men with grown children who are independent.

Gone – We talked about the fact that we were in different stages of our lives and stopped dating.

Mr. False Witness was an attorney in the Washington, D.C., region. We had flirted on the dating app, enjoyed our conversations over several phone calls, and then he asked me out to dinner. I was new to the area and not yet familiar with the local favorites, so he selected a restaurant called the Peking Gourmet Inn located in Falls Church, Virginia. At first glance, you'd think the place was a hole-in-the-wall diner because it was in a strip mall. When I walked into the restaurant, I noticed the white tablecloths and the walls covered with pictures of famous people both past and present. The meal was amazing, including the artistry exhibited by the servers as they carved up their specialty, Peking duck, right before our eyes tableside.

Having had a bit of experience with dating apps, I observed that some people were not always truthful on their profiles. As we were sipping on our after-dinner drinks, I took the opportunity and offered him a proverbial "get out of jail free card," letting him know that if there was anything not truthful on his dating profile, if he shared it now, he could use this card and there would be no consequences. He said everything was truthful, and we left it at that.

Mr. False Witness and I had been dating for a few months when he called me, asking how adventurous I was. He wanted to take a trip to the Fiji Islands and asked if I wanted to go with him. I said, "I'm in." Two weeks later, there we were at Dulles International Airport, sitting in our plane on the tarmac, waiting for takeoff. His previous passport expired, and he had a new shiny one in his hands and like a new toy, he wanted me to see it.

I opened his passport to see his picture and much to my surprise his birth year was very different than what he had placed on his dating profile. I turned to him and said, "You lied to me." He looked confused and asked, "What?" I showed him his passport page, pointed out his birth year, and said, "You lied to me about your age." **Mr. False Witness** began to tell me that there was no way I would have dated him had I known his real age. I said, "Well, now we'll never know because you did not afford me the chance; you made that decision for me."

We recovered and had a fabulous time on the islands. We stayed at a lovely resort right on the water and hired a driver to take us away from regular tourist haunts in favor of the local villages. One day the driver took us to his mom's home located in another village across the island. Her home had been constructed Bure style. This means that it was built with anything they could get their hands on, tie a rope around, or stack together like corrugated metal, plywood, or traditional two-by-four lumber. Their home was rectangular in shape, and when we walked through the front door into the living space, we were standing on the same exposed dirt as we had outside the front door.

The driver's mother and sister were very proud to show us their home and animals, and they wanted to share a bite to eat with us. His sister took me out back where we gathered fresh milk from their goats and brought it back to her mother. The household stove and oven combination were constructed with brick and was approximately ten feet away from the house. The mother had already built a wood fire in an open space under the stove area. Her stove was made using metal electric range burner drip bowls in which she placed the milk. Before you knew it, we each had glasses of warm goat milk and warm honey cakes in our hands as we sat in their living room enjoying their gracious hospitality.

Another day, our driver took us to a village known for spearfishing. He introduced us to a local tribesman, and we literally stood thigh-high in water with a spear in hand and threw them like darts into the water at the fish swimming near us. It took some time to figure out how to throw the spear ahead of the fish anticipating the direction and speed both the fish and the spear would travel. Once we got the hang of it, we caught six fish that afternoon, took them back to our resort, cooked them up outside on an open flame grill, and ate them while sitting on an old wooden picnic bench staring at the blue ocean water.

Brief – We were good at being activity partners, but no real chemistry existed between us, and we were honest with each other about it.

Brilliant – When people show you who they are, believe them. Don't wear your rose-colored glasses and think that they will change or that you will change them. This character trait of secret-keeping or not telling the truth was a red flag for me because it is an unhealthy practice in relationships. If he was afraid to tell the truth about his birthdate, something that anyone can easily learn on the internet, imagine how hard it would have been for him to tell the truth when it came to real matters of the heart.

Gone – Since we were flying from D.C. through Los Angeles and on to Fiji outbound, I had already booked my flight coming back to get off the plane in Los Angeles so I could visit family in California. When we arrived at LAX, we walked through customs together and said our goodbyes. I went to pick up my luggage, and he went to catch his next plane back to D.C. That was the last time we saw each other.

Mr. Universe was an architectural engineer and a deep-sea diver who had traveled to many of the best diving locations in the world. He was a member of the National Association of Underwater Instructors, and although I had never been diving, he wanted me to get certified so we could

107

dive together. I had light claustrophobia and experienced mild anxiety when anything was placed over my face. The first hurdle would be to get me comfortable with wearing a scuba mask and regulator.

Mr. Universe was a good teacher and extremely patient with me in the shallow end of the pool as I placed the scuba gear on my face and kneeled under the water, testing my ability to stay there without panicking. After about forty minutes of above-water and below-water experimentation, I gained more confidence. I was able to move to the deep end of the pool and stay under for longer periods of time. By the end of the evening, we were underwater side by side moving back and forth across the length of the pool like it had always been that way.

We both were climbing the career ladders in our respective industries. **Mr. Universe** had never been married and lived in an apartment. I owned my own home and had invited him over one evening for dinner. After dinner was over, we went outside to stargaze. He was knowledgeable about the constellations and pointed out the ones he recognized.

While staring at the stars, I made a comment about the beauty of the universe. He immediately replied, asking me, "How do you know it is not multi?" And just like that, with one question he expanded my thinking and my curiosity. I had only been exposed to the term "universe." I had not been exposed to the term "multiverse."

Brief – In a short period of time, he exposed me to underwater adventures in diving and expanded my curiosity about physics, space, and time.

Brilliant – Through dating someone that was "not my type" and stepping outside my comfort zone, I was splendidly rewarded. He introduced me to several new experiences, increased my self-awareness beyond my fears, and altered several of my preferences in men.

Gone – We both were clear that we were married to our careers, and neither of us was willing at that time to give them up. He was offered an opportunity in another state at the same time I took an opportunity to work for my company overseas.

Michelin Star Man

How will you know if he is your **Michelin Star Man?** The Michelin Guides are a series of guidebooks that identify gastronomic destinations around the world. These guides have been published since 1904, and they inspire restaurant chefs and owners to be the most innovative and creative in their field. The guide awards up to three Michelin stars for excellence to a select few restaurant establishments. The Michelin Star System awards a one-star rating to a very good restaurant in its category, a two-star rating rewards excellent cuisine worth a detour; and a three-star rating promises exceptional cuisine worth a special journey.

As you sift and sort through the men on your dating app, evaluate the men you have dated, and consider your preferences in men and what you want to experience with men inside of a relationship. Sort those preferences and relationship experiences into three categories:

1. One star = Very good, promising, in his own category
2. Two stars = Excellent, worth a detour or going out of your way to explore
3. Three stars = Exceptional, worth a special journey

Approaching the dating game wondering if *he will like you or want you* is ass backward. Go into the dating game with curiosity, exploration, and self-development of your relationship skills in mind. Give up forcing the relationship to become something. Once you stop forcing it into a specific form, it could become everything and more than you imagined, causing you to grow and expand your relationship abilities in ways you never expected.

Consider sharing your heart only to those who are exceptional and worthy of a special journey.

Introspection Questions

1. How many men have you dated in your lifetime?
2. Have you ever allowed yourself to date more than one man at a time? Have you given yourself permission to date more than one man at a time? If not, why not?
3. Think back on your dating relationships.
   a. Write down the characteristics that you appreciated about each man.
   b. Write down the characteristics you wish each man would have embodied.
   c. Take each dating experience and identify what you learned about yourself and how you grew because of the experience. Can you identify any opportunities you may have missed to grow and develop your relationship abilities?
   d. Take each man one by one and jot down the characteristics that you did not like and prefer not to have in your future relationships. After you write those down, then answer why you did not like those characteristics.
   e. Which relationships did you allow to go on when you knew they were already over? Why did you allow that relationship to stay in your life?
   f. How many new relationship skills have you developed with your dating activities? Acknowledge yourself for your self-development and appreciate the men who assisted in helping you develop your new abilities.
4. Create a comprehensive list of the criteria for the partner and partnership that you seek.
5. Take your partner and partnership criteria list and identify what items on your list are negotiable and which ones are non-negotiable. (For example: He must be into keeping his body fit, must be nicotine-free, must be kind to me in public and in private settings, must be generous with his love, must be happy, and manage his well-being).
6. Have you ever asked a potential partner what their partner and partnership criteria is and what their non-negotiables are?

CHAPTER 9

KISS AND WAKE UP

My final dress fitting was completed, he owned his own tux, and everything else had been planned and paid for, including our honeymoon in the British Territory of the Western Caribbean. Our family and friends had their plane tickets in hand, hotels booked, and their wedding attire packed. Many wonderful gifts had already been received, thank-you notes written and ready to be placed in the mail. Only a few last-minute wedding details remained for me to take care of, the most crucial of which was to *call off the wedding*.

SAY WHAT?

Yes, call off the wedding.

This story begins with my company moving my daughter and me to another city where a new job opportunity inside the company and a new city adventure awaited. As many times as my companies have moved my daughter and me, we learned to find new ways of getting involved in the community so we could make friends and make it our home for as long as we might be there.

Mr. Knight in Shining Armor and I met in a community theater group where he was playing a leading role in the production, and I had a supporting role. We flirted backstage one night and he seriously caught me off guard by complimenting me, stating that he loved my legs. Then he asked me out on a date.

I had taken ballet lessons for years, was an athlete since junior high school, was involved in various sports, and then became a cheerleader in both my junior and senior years in high school. I was described as "big-boned" by various family members, had built up seriously defined double muscles in my calves from the years of ballet and sports, and was teased by other students about the size of my calves. This made me extremely self-conscious to the point where I would wear mostly pants instead of dresses so that no one could see my legs.

As we dated and I got to know **Mr. Knight in Shining Armor**, I learned he was a business owner and very well-known in the city. He invited me to his business several times, and eventually we teamed up on new creative ideas to capitalize on and expand his already successful business venture. It was fun to work side by side, shoulder to shoulder, and experience this collaborative relationship we were developing. We truly valued each other's contributions and complementary perspectives.

During this same time frame, I had enrolled in a personal and professional development curriculum created by a coaching organization designed to produce new possibilities and breakthroughs in a person's life. I had signed up for one of their four-month leadership courses designed to expand a person's capacity for making a difference on a broader scale.

Each participant was assigned a coach for the duration of the course and the first thing we were asked to do was design a project in alignment with our passion and commitment to serving others. The project had to include teaming up with others and needed to have an impact on more than two hundred people.

One of the ways this leadership development course enabled its participants' transformation was to have them create a "possibility statement" for their leadership expression. Bold Leadership and Abundance for Everyone was the possibility statement I created. This declaration would be my new compass for creating the required project, its associated activities, and community impact.

During that four-month course, I did not ask, "What would Heather do?" Every time I had to make decisions or take the next step, I asked myself and my team "What would Bold Leadership and Abundance for Everyone do next?" I learned very quickly that living up to a possibility was catalyzing, transformative, and more than personally and professionally rewarding. It was almost transcendent.

A few of my friends wanted to take the business skills they had developed in their corporate jobs and explore how they could work for themselves and put those talents to work in service to their communities. Bold Leadership and Abundance for Everyone came up with the project idea to create the state's First Annual Women Supporting Women in Entrepreneurship Conference, a conference designed to bring together the various components of what it takes to start, run, and maintain your own business. This conference would be led by women in support of other women.

Since he was already a skilled entrepreneur, I was very excited to share this newly created idea with **Mr. Knight in Shining Armor**. He was very supportive of the project and then showed me the underutilized office space located in his business operation. He generously offered it, free of charge, to me and the five women collaborating with me on this endeavor.

Mr. Knight in Shining Armor was business-minded and knew how to approach the project objectively using his analytical and critical-thinking capabilities. He was also in tune with his intuition and had the ability to understand things quickly without the need for conscious reasoning. I saw this balance of right- and left-brain capacity as a foundational match between us. That foundation coupled with the mutual professional support we gave each other versus the professional competition present in some of my past love relationships was extremely attractive.

Mr. Knight in Shining Armor continued to surprise me with his eclectic and generous nature, which ranged from architectural model building and art collecting to his love for European pastries and charitable food and Bible distribution. One sunny summer afternoon, he took me on a long country-backroads ride on his motorcycle. After a few hours, we came back to his house and there was a new model he had built sitting on the dining room table.

He could not wait to show me his newly created architectural model. It was an elaborate medieval castle complete with high walls, turrets on each corner of the castle, and included a prayer chapel. Hidden inside the model castle was a box with a ring, and just like that, we were engaged.

The next motorcycle ride we took was to visit a large piece of property he owned. That is when he shared his plan for taking that model and building a real castle on his land. We decided to invite our friends and family out to the property for a groundbreaking and land-blessing ceremony, then announce our engagement to everyone in attendance and share a champagne toast with our loved ones.

A decade before *Shark Tank*'s first episode, our band of six women were busy executing the activities entailed with hosting a large conference to support women in entrepreneurship. None of us had ever been engaged in something of this magnitude, so we just kept asking what Bold Leadership and Abundance for Everyone would do, and it led us into multiple, almost miraculous experiences.

1. We engaged with the state's business development center for women, collaborating with them to create twenty-five scholarships that would be awarded at the end of the conference to women with a clear idea and vision for creating a business that would benefit the community. The scholarships enabled the women to attend a two-month business development course, educating them in business plan development and execution.
2. We reached out to women business leaders all over the city of every ethnicity to see if they would be interested in stepping on stage to share their inspiring message, tools, and entrepreneurial success stories with other women.

3. We contacted vendors and provided them with opportunities to market their products and services in exchange for contributions to the twenty-five scholarships to be awarded at the end of the conference.

4. We contacted businesses and offered them opportunities to be featured sponsors in the conference brochure and catalogued every women's organization across the state in the back of the conference brochure to ensure that women knew what support resources they had at their fingertips.

5. A bold leadership move was sending one-page letters to five nationally well-known women, requesting that they consider being our keynote speaker. Marianne Williamson, the author of thirteen books, spiritual leader, and political activist, answered with a resounding "YES!" as she was inspired by our efforts and committed to the same vision. She noted that her keynote speaking services would be gratis and all we needed to do was purchase her plane ticket and transport her from and to the airport the day of the conference.

Now that we had all the details lined up, we created the flyers, brochures, and press release information, and targeted every newspaper, radio station spot, and media outlet we could identify to get the word out and the ticket sales coming in.

We reached out to our friends who worked behind the community theater scenes creating the backdrops for each play. They too wanted to be part of the event and they big-heartedly gave their time and talents to creating the stage settings for the women's conference.

Like many others before me, I was doubtful about the claims that this transformational organization made about its ability to create breakthroughs and new possibilities in my life. I thought that its claims were a bit audacious at the time, but through the power of the tools and distinctions provided during this leadership course, I was catapulted onto radio shows, TV stations, and news interviews, handling them with confidence and eloquence in my communications, thanks to the continual support of my program coach.

There were several times I and my colleagues were awestruck by the continual outpouring of kindness and generosity from women that flowed like a river of angels cooperating with us in support of this event. Assistance came from the most unsuspecting places at the most needed of times.

While occupied with this project, I was still working a full-time job, taking care of my grade school-aged daughter, and planning a wedding with **Mr. Knight in Shining Armor**. The closer it got to our wedding date, the more revealing he was about his religious activities and beliefs. He spoke frequently to me about accepting Jesus as my Lord and Savior, noting that I needed to be saved.

The day of the conference was fast approaching. My original idea and vision became the team's vision, and together the six of us loved that vision into a reality. The conference attracted more than six hundred participants, an auditorium full of vendors, a day filled with amazing women speakers, and ended with awarding twenty-five scholarships to deserving women who would, no doubt, develop their business plans, start their businesses, and pay it forward in their own communities.

There is no way to describe the excitement and energy embodied by the six hundred attendees who came from six different states on that day. The wave of enthusiasm was exhilarating, creating a magical feeling for the six of us as if we were floating on air the entire time while staying focused on delivering the conference sessions and activities.

I was one of the speakers that day and my talk was titled "How to Be a Vision Keeper." There was no nervousness in my body or concern for myself or how I looked. All that was present for myself and all the other speakers **was our contribution to others.**

We had a driver pick up Marianne Williamson from the airport. She asked the driver to take her to an HIV/AIDS hospice facility where she could provide her compassionate caring support to its patients in the last phase of their lives here on earth. When she arrived at the conference, she was backstage engaged in talking with my daughter, and after she gave her inspiring keynote, I was privileged to sit by her side while she autographed hundreds of books. I was in awe of her tireless energy and unwavering presence as she held the hand of every attendee and listened to them as if they were the only person in the room. I knew then that I was in the presence of a master who had mastered the art of being present.

Toward the end of the conference, the joy of the day began to dissipate when it appeared that **Mr. Knight in Shining Armor** was envious of the limelight the team was receiving. **Mr. Knight in Shining Armor** did not seem pleased with the attention I was giving to the conference attendees, and he kept vying for my attention and trying to pull me away. My daughter is very observant, and she too became aware that he was not involved in being of help, not sharing in the happiness of the day, or actively celebrating the overall success of the conference or the team. The contrast between that *love- and joy-filled day* and the *Knight* smacked me right in the face.

Fairy-Tale Prince Saving You?

Did you grow up watching or reading about the various Disney princesses? Were you one of those little girls who dreamed of going to Disneyland to visit Cinderella's Castle or Disney World so you could meet those princesses in person? Perhaps you dressed up like a princess for Halloween or wore those princess dresses until they were ragged. Maybe you pretended that your Prince Charming would come and kiss you, wake you up, and take you away to his castle, or at the very least his house.

It has been more than three hundred years since the original Sleeping Beauty story was written in 1697. *Sleeping Beauty* (Princess Aurora) is a classic fairy tale about a princess who is cursed by an evil witch who is angry that she was not invited to the princess's christening party. The curse is that Sleeping Beauty will sleep for one hundred years with her deep sleep ending and the curse broken when her *betrothed*, Prince Phillip, kisses her and wakes her up. At her christening ceremony, her father, King

Hubert, arranged her marriage to Prince Philip, the son of his best friend, King Stefan, so that the two kings could unite their kingdoms. Yes, promising his daughter's hand in marriage as a business transaction.

Snow White is so beautiful that another woman can't stand to have her around. The other woman just happens to be the queen and Snow White's evil stepmother. Snow White's stepmother sends one of her henchmen to do her dirty work by ordering him to kill Snow White. That is some serious jealousy! The henchman is not successful, so the queen takes matters into her own hands. The queen poisons Snow White, causing her to fall into a comatose state, a spell that can only be broken by Prince Charming's true-love kiss, or in this case, Prince Florian's.

We take some of these childhood dreams and turn them into our adult fantasies supporting a $78- billion-a-year wedding industry in the United States alone. We bring our own fairy-tale versions to life when we plan our weddings, from the wedding gown and saying, "I do," to the shoes and inviting hundreds of people to dance and dine for a weekend or longer of celebrating, and then we fly, drive, or ride off to live our version of happily ever after.

In the specific fairy tales of *Sleeping Beauty, Cinderella,* and *Snow White,* a prince was imagined and created to save each of these women. Snow White was saved from her wicked stepmother, Cinderella was saved from her hard work and servitude to her stepmother and stepsisters, and Sleeping Beauty was saved from an evil witch's curse of instant death on her sixteenth birthday.

I know that there have been times in my life when I wished for someone to "save me" from whatever circumstances seemed insurmountable at the time. When I worked through those circumstances, I became even more cognizant of my own resilience and inner strength. If I had allowed someone to "save me" from those challenging circumstances, it would have resulted in disabling me by creating a dependence upon them and robbing me of knowing my own depth and capacity.

When I started dating **Mr. Knight in Shining Armor**, I was not a helpless damsel in distress waiting or looking for a man to save or rescue me. His armor was a shiny dazzling distraction with all the trappings of a fairy tale and fortune that got me caught up in *his dream* for a little while. It did not take long to wake up and remember the future *I* was interested in creating. I did not want a relationship with someone who thought I was "broken" and needed fixing nor was I interested in seeing someone else as "broken" and needing fixing. That would hardly be the foundation for a partnership. I was interested and intrigued by the possibility of equality in a partnership created out of pure choice, not neediness or the need to fix someone else.

Letting Go in Love #Adulting

One way to know that you are beginning to develop the ability to consciously create your love story is that you will slow down and avoid destroying another person and the love you created just because it might not have the happily-ever-after ending either of you desired. You will also become more adept at getting still, asking yourself the tough questions, listening to your honest answers, and proceeding with truthful heart-centered actions.

I asked myself, what was it that *didn't feel quite right*? What was *not fully in alignment between the two of us*? The answers were very clear and pointed me in the right direction. I needed to have a heart-to-heart conversation with **Mr. Knight in Shining Armor.**

We met in a quiet place where we could be present to each other. I shared with him that it didn't feel quite right when he kept religiously trying to "save me." I shared with him that I felt he believed I was going to hell and the constant experience of my partner wanting to change me was not a solid foundation for our marriage. As we continued to talk about our thinking and beliefs, we agreed that we were not spiritually aligned, nor were we moving in the same direction. Together we talked about what we loved and appreciated about each other. Together we determined that getting married was not the right thing for either of us. We discussed how we would tell our family and friends, handle gift returning and other details that come with calling off a wedding. He was truly relieved and thanked me for having the inner strength to begin the conversation. Then the unthinkable happened. He said, "You know, the honeymoon is already paid for. What do you think about enjoying a vacation together?" We did just that!

It is common to take one or two years to plan a wedding. Many changes can take place during this one-to-two-year planning time due to family; financial, and religious decisions need to be addressed. Perhaps the challenges come when one of the parties does not get involved or won't deal with the challenges or tough decisions to be made. As you prepare to walk down the aisle, are you still the same people you thought you were when you got engaged a year or eighteen months ago?

Next time a relationship challenge comes up, consider taking the time to create new possibilities for yourself and others. Ask yourself, in this situation **what would love do?** *In this moment* **how would love respond?** *What would love say to me and/or to my potential partner about this challenge, problem, or need?*

Introspection Questions

1. What relationships have you been in where you felt that he wanted to change you and what were the changes he wanted you to make? How did/does that make you feel?
2. What relationship have you been in where you wanted him to change? What changes did you want him to make? Why did you want him to make those changes?
3. In what ways were you/are you his project?
4. In what ways were you/are you his partner?
5. How were you/are you the supporting role in the relationship?
6. How were you/are you the lead role in the relationship?
7. Have you ever dimmed your light or hidden your talents so as not to outshine him?
8. Do you allow yourself to shine as bright or brighter than him?

9. What happens when the spotlight is on you and not on him? On him and not you?
10. What are the things you like to do together?
11. What are the things you like to do on your own?
12. In your current or past relationships, is/was there any unhealthy competition?
13. In your current or past relationships, what complementary skills and talents do/did each of you bring to the relationship?
14. Has there ever been a time you did the work, and he took the credit?
15. How does he support you personally?
16. How does he support you professionally?
17. How do you support him personally?
18. How do you support him professionally?
19. In what instances do you not feel supported?
20. In what instances might he not feel supported?
21. Think of five different ways in which you could ask him to support you.
22. How does he celebrate your successes?
23. How do you celebrate his successes?
24. Where and how are you aligned or not aligned in your thinking and beliefs about finances, family, friends, food, fitness, alcohol, spirituality, religion, culture, television time, music, and books, etc.
25. How and in what relationship(s) did you fall for the prestige of his job, his things, or his lifestyle and end up captive in his castle?
26. When have you had the thought that you wish someone would "save" you?
27. What did you want them to save you from? Your lack of finances or poverty, like Cinderella? Your wicked stepmother or family?
28. Are you in a relationship that is not what you imagined or signed up for? What would it look like if you were to talk with that person and discuss how you both could let each other go with love?

29. Great athletes hire coaches to ensure they are playing at the top of their game because coaches see what they can't see. Have you ever considered hiring a coach to ensure you play at the top of your abilities when it comes to matters of the heart? If not, why not?

CHAPTER 10

NO MORE FLINCHING

Have you ever been involved in an *office romance* or gossiped about one?

It is more common than you may realize. In a February 2020 article entitled "Workplace Romances: Getting to the Heart of the Matter" by Kathy Gurchiek, which appeared on the Society for Human Resource Management (SHRM) website, more than half of the organization's survey respondents admitted to having romantic feelings for a co-worker and almost 25 percent have asked a colleague out on a date.

The rules have changed quite a bit since my workplace rendezvous, as many companies have put workplace romance policies in place to create respectful cultures and they educate and remind management of this fact on a regular basis as these relationships could create serious legal ramifications for everyone involved.

If you are currently engaged in a workplace romance or think that you may want to jump in that dating pool, you may want to read the February 2019 *Harvard Business Review*'s story "How to Approach an Office Romance (and How Not To)" by Amy Gallo. It is packed with relevant considerations that will surely enable mindfulness in this lover's lane.

Now that we have talked a bit about the current state of office romance, let me tell you about an experience I had approximately three decades ago.

The company **Mr. Office Romance** and I worked for had the motto of *Work Hard Play Harder*, and we were already two days into the four-day professional development conference that included live music, dancing, and open bars every night. With over a thousand attendees, it was a human resource leader's nightmare for at least ninety-six hours.

We were heavily celebrating our firm's accomplishments, and I was personally partying because earlier in the evening, I had received the CEO's Annual Achievement Award, which was the highest honor for a consultant in our firm. I admittedly had quite a bit to drink. At 2:00 a.m., I was not able to walk a straight line back up to my hotel room but still managed to find my way.

Bright and early came my wake-up call from the hotel receptionist ensuring that I got to the conference session I was leading that morning. I, like many others' attending the conference, was in no condition to retain any educational information being delivered, much less stand in front of a room and present the material.

It didn't take long for me to wake up. I felt like death warmed over and yet, even with my hangover hurting every cell in my body, I didn't flinch, I rolled over in my bed and asked **Mr. Office Romance**, "When were you going to tell me about your other girlfriend?"

About last night, there is a little detail I left out. During the evening's social event, a colleague came up to me and asked me where **Mr. Office Romance** was. When I said I didn't know, she unwittingly said she had seen him earlier with his girlfriend but couldn't find him now and she needed to speak with him.

Mr. Office Romance and I met while working together on an intense, large-scale project. He was an intelligent and accomplished professional—kind, calm, and well-traveled. He was a great listener and generous, including the way he shared his time and knowledge when asked. He had a pleasant relationship with the mother of his grown children who were living on their own.

Mr. Office Romance was enormously thoughtful in his gift-giving, and he continually created fun destinations for our stress-free traveling together. One New Year's Eve, he booked a corner suite overlooking Times Square in New York City. We got dressed up, had dinner in an upscale restaurant, and then went back to our luxurious room. With the huge, picturesque windows, we could see every sparkling light and celebratory hopeful person below as we toasted to the new year with champagne while we watched the ball drop.

Mr. Office Romance planned beach trips for us in the United States on both the East and West Coasts, a trip to the Bahamas, and multiple trips to other Caribbean islands. He took me on my first seaplane ride to a Caribbean island where we snorkeled, ate cheeseburgers in paradise, and placed bets on the crab races. Who knew you could buy your own crab, name it, bet on it, and win a bottle of Caribbean rum for coming in second place?

It was very refreshing for me to be in a relationship with **Mr. Office Romance**. He did not try to control anything I did. He was not critical, he did not tell me what to do, how to look, what clothes to wear, how to speak, or try to tell me whom I could or couldn't spend my time with. He was even supportive of my personal desire to expand my spiritual abilities and, although it was not his path to follow, he was supportive of my journey.

This potential *Mr. Right* created a safe space where I could just be me without fear of being judged or criticized. I was able to let my shoulders relax, I could express myself freely, and for the first time, a man could touch my face without me flinching. For this relationship of healing, I will forever be grateful.

While **Mr. Office Romance** and I were working together professionally, neither of us had plans to tell our colleagues that we were seeing each other personally. As road warrior consultants, we knew that it was just a matter of time before we would be assigned somewhere else across the country on new projects.

The path to more consciously creating your love story will support you in revealing the places where you may have allowed your love for another person to blind you. The path to more consciously creating your love story will expose the places where you may have unconsciously extended trust as a replacement for taking risks and asking intimate questions that would offer you clarity and support you in avoiding being a victim of love.

Mr. Office Romance was not expecting that I would learn about his already having a girlfriend. Seriously, what are the chances amid a business conference filled with over a thousand attendees? The chances are .001 percent. He was obviously banking on the 99.999 percent chance that I would never know she existed. Oops, the cat is out of the bag! What happened next?

Since this story began, did it cross your mind that he *cheated* on me or *betrayed* me, or *lied* to me? Were you rooting for me to go tell the "*other woman*," expose him, and get revenge? Perhaps you considered that maybe I was the "*other woman?*" At any time, did you think that he was a "*player*," or did you hear Britney Spears singing, "Womanizer, woman-womanizer, you're a womanizer" in your head?

I had progressed enough along my own love story path that even with a hangover I was able to roll over in my bed and asked the man in it, "When were you going to tell me about your other girlfriend?"

Believing that he was "caught" or "busted," this potential *Mr. Right* started to squirm and stammer as he pulled the bed covers over his body in an effort to use those hotel sheets for protection during this vulnerable encounter. **Mr. Office Romance** quickly launched into excuse creating and I stopped him as soon as I could, creating a pattern interrupt to get his attention so we could attempt to have a more conscious conversation. I got the conversation started by saying, "We never made any promises to each other," and we talked more over the next several weeks.

When truth has the opportunity to get air, breathe, and be heard, it will bring you deeper realizations about yourself and the love partner you have chosen, especially when you have no resistance to hearing what the truth wants to reveal to you. Then you can determine what is best for you and make the choices that more consciously create the love story you desire.

We uncovered and clarified what was true about our relationship, separating the facts from the story or drama.

- We had no relationship agreements in place.
- Neither one of us had ever broached the topic of dating each other exclusively.
- Neither of us asked questions about the potential of one or both of us having multiple sexual partners.
- We had no discussions about each other's monogamy or non-monogamy relationship preferences.
- He was dating one other woman.
- I was dating only him.
- We loved and cared for each other and were very comfortable in each other's company.
- Both of us were career professionals, and neither of us had plans to change.
- We knew how to have fun together whether wearing jeans or cocktail attire.
- We traveled well together and enjoyed turquoise seas and warm-weather climates.
- We both had cultivated friendly relationships with our former spouses and our children were young adults.

I intentionally took time for self-reflection so I could get honest with myself about what I did/did not want right then and further clarify my relationship preferences for the type of partnership my heart and soul desired in the future.

- I noticed I was not upset that he was dating two women at the same time.
- Why was I not upset? At this time in my life, I was interested in being free to do whatever I wanted, when I wanted.
- I wasn't interested in getting married, and I did not want a man pushing me or our relationship into a more committed state.

- I was enjoying the experience of infrequently dating the same person. It kept things fresh and kept me from having to make any commitments.
- I appreciated the wake-up call at the conference reminding me to bring more consciousness to my relationships, get curious, don't assume, and **ask more questions.**
- I wanted at least every other weekend to myself to pursue things of interest to me.
- I clarified how important it was for me to continue developing my spiritual gifts and not be distracted.

When something happens in your love story that is not optimal, it is time for self-reflection so that you can see where your hands may not be on the wheel steering your love bus, or where there might be an opportunity to create your love story more consciously by identifying what was missing from your conscious awareness.

In this relationship with **Mr. Office Romance**, I assumed he was dating only me. Let's define assumption. *Assumption is a thing that is accepted as true without proof.* I assumed that he was a man with a preference for dating only one woman at a time. Notice I did not say monogamous. The origin of that word in the Greek language is *monos* (single) *gamos* (marriage), which is the practice or state of being married to one person at a time. It is also used to describe the practice or state of having a sexual relationship with only one partner.

In the beginning of this relationship, I may also have allowed myself to be "love-blind" by giving my emotional senses more weight than my sense of objectivity. If I would have taken the time to objectively look at the early-relationship activities, it may have raised my awareness of the fact that he had been on the road for years, meeting women at company or networking events and hotel bars, with opportunities for hotel room rendezvous in their room or his. **Mr. Office Romance** met with me secretly on a business project and, looking at it objectively, I would have considered that he had done this in the past and with him being committed to staying on the road, might do this again in the future.

Because I was not interested in being in a long-term committed relationship at the time, I was asleep at my love bus wheel and not asking questions. I never asked him if he was dating only me or if I was his only sexual partner. I also did not ask him about his personal relationship preferences, his relationship beliefs, his gender orientation, or his sexual partner preferences.

In this game of love, let's define a few other terms that tend to get used without exact clarity, starting with the definition of the word *cheating*. According to *Webster's Dictionary*, it means to break a promise made to someone, such as one's wife or husband by having sex with someone else.

I recently spoke with two different women who each had a "cheating partner" experience, and they approached their experience in different ways.

The first woman had been dating the same guy for three months, but they had never slept with each other, and both were active on dating sites. She shared with me that when she learned he had gone out on a date with another woman, she yelled at him, accusing him of cheating on her, betraying her, and lying to her, and she ended the relationship.

The second woman was married, and even though she knew her husband was not committed to monogamy, she thought if she kept seeing the best in him, he would change. She shared that she had been scrolling through her husband's phone and found a new number she did not recognize. She called the new number and talked with the woman and learned that she had been on a date with her husband earlier that week. She then sent a text message to several other women in her husband's phone, telling them about each other in order to expose his extramarital activities.

If you have a cheating partner, you could spend your time and energy focused on him and what he is doing or getting revenge. You could also choose to spend your precious energy on yourself by being still and asking yourself:

- What am I getting out of the relationship?
- What am I not getting out of the relationship?

- What is the next best move that will take care of me and my needs?

Seek your inner knowing and see if he is truly a Mr. Right or a Mr. Right Now. Seek and listen to your inner knowing to gain clarity on what you prefer or don't prefer in your perfect partnership or relationship.

No matter what the dictionary has to say about it, define what cheating means to you:

- When it comes to cheating, how do you and how does your partner define it?
- Is cheating when your partner looks at another person with a "wandering" eye?
- Is cheating when your partner is physically touching or kissing another person?
- Is cheating when your partner is engaged in online dating activities?

When you explore your thinking and beliefs about cheating, the answers you learn may surprise you and your partner.

Looking at my relationship through the lens of *Webster*'s meaning of *cheating* revealed that involves breaking a promise made to someone, such as one's wife or husband by having sex with someone else.

Mr. Office Romance and I were not married to each other, nor were we married to other people. When we began dating, we did not promise that we would only date each other, nor did we make a promise that we would only have sex with each other.

I did not falsely accuse him of cheating on me. In fact, I was grateful for the wake-up call that led to rich and revealing conversations. He planned to continue being a road warrior, traveling 100 percent of the time for business, and he desired to find a woman who would settle down with him so they could grow old together. During this time in my life, I was not interested in settling down. I was also not willing to keep dating someone who was non-monogamous.

We agreed that we were traveling in different directions and ended our dating relationship.

Introspection Questions:

1. What do you want? If you do not have what you want, what questions might you ask to have the love relationship you desire?
2. Where might you be "love-blind" in your current relationship or where might you have been "love-blind" in your previous relationships?
3. If you are in a relationship, what agreements do you have with each another? Are they assumed or have you discussed them together and come to an agreement?
4. If you are dating someone, do you have any agreement to date only each other? Do you want to date only him? Does he want to date only you? Are you dating only him? Is he dating only you?
5. Are you having sex with only him? Is he having sex with only you? What discussions have you had about the number of sexual partners either or both of you agree to?
6. What type of relationship do you want? What type of relationship does he want?
7. Do you want to be monogamous? Does he want to be monogamous?
8. How much together time do you want? How much together time does he want?
9. What does cheating mean to you? What does cheating mean to him?
10. Do you read his text messages, scroll through call logs to see whom he has been talking to, or look at his online history to see what internet sites he visits?

11. Where might you be assuming things in your relationship?
12. Based upon the assumptions you uncover, what questions should you be asking?
13. Have you ever accused someone of "cheating" when in fact you had no agreements in place?
14. Have you been or are you currently in a relationship with a man who is non-monogamous? Why did you or do you stay in that relationship?
15. Is the relationship you are in fulfilling the love story you desire for yourself?
16. In what ways do you appreciate Mr. Right Now, for any contributions he has made to you along your love story journey?
17. In what ways can you show gratitude for the clarity Mr. Right Now, has brought you in refining your partnership or relationship preferences?

CHAPTER 11

HEART BREAK

Love does not care what form it takes. Love is love whether you are part of a family sharing love, friends or dating sharing love, engaged or married loving each other, divorced and being loving toward your former spouse, or loving yourself.

If you looked at the entirety of my love story over the last thirty years, you would see that I have been married, single, or dating on and off for the entire time. During those three decades of being married, single, or dating, I don't ever recall consciously choosing to practice self-love. Those words did not exist in my vocabulary because media, family examples, cultural and religious influences for thousands of years have depicted a life of sacrifice for me as a woman. This involved sacrificing myself and my needs in service to household chores and child-rearing, foregoing my education or career in support of my husband's, forfeiting my authentic voice because I had to walk that thin line of not speaking too much or risk being perceived as aggressive, or not speaking up enough and being judged as ineffectual or weak.

My friends and I did not spend time consciously thinking or talking about self-love. I don't remember ever taking the time to become more self-aware by deliberately exploring my personality traits or what I liked and did not like. I don't remember dedicating time to consciously considering *just* me, without taking a child, my job, a man, or another family member into consideration, or considering societal and other people's opinions.

Like Dry January or Sober October, I needed a program like March Without Men or Self-Love September or Dating Myself December. I decided that instead of the Twelve Days of Christmas, I would commit to Twelve Months of Sacred Self-Love.

I gave myself, and my heart, a break for an entire year.

Two of my friends did more than give their heart a break. They quit the idea of happily ever, both for very different reasons:

One friend of mine in her late forties had been through two divorces and emphatically expressed that she was "damaged goods" and resigned herself to being loved for the rest of her life only by her dogs, even though this wasn't what she really wanted.

Her interpretation of being divorced was that she was a failure. She judged herself harshly and imposed her own sentence as self-punishment. She chose to remain bitter and victimized by the men she had selected to be in a relationship with while refusing to see the part she played in being attracted to them or attracting them to her. It was difficult to watch my extremely talented, kind, generous, and beautiful friend close the doors on her heart and assuming a life of solitude when she could have what she really wanted.

The other friend, in her early fifties, had been through one divorce, had experienced her marriage as enriching, and decided she could still connect with men in vital ways without marriage or cohabitating. She experienced so much freedom by turning her energy 100 percent toward her life and the things that brought her joy. From what I witnessed, she loved having her own place, her alone time, and found her friendships to be invaluable and enriching to her life. She shared frequently that she loved having the time to pursue her interests and hobbies as opposed to giving her time to more than her fair share of household chores or to the caretaking others.

I wasn't sure what would be waiting for me at the end of my one-year sacred self-love program. Would I powerfully be choosing me or powerfully choosing me and partnership? Regardless of which direction I went in the end, my journey and my life were gold medals worth pursuing.

Much like an Olympic athlete ensures they are operating at their personal best, I was interested in healthy functioning and enhancing my well-being. Aristotle is recognized for stating that "knowing yourself is the beginning of all wisdom." I wanted to gain more wisdom, and I was willing to do the work involved in looking at myself and my love story over the years.

Have you ever taken a dedicated amount of time for self-love? I was not sure where to begin, but as soon as I made the commitment to do it, avenues to explore began to show up. As I look back, I could see that my sacred self-love journey involved remembering my accomplishments, reviewing my point of attraction, revising my approach, rebuilding, and rejuvenating my emotional, physical, mental, and spiritual foundations.

Your sacred self-love path will be unique to you, and it will start when you are ready and make the commitment to choose *yourself*.

When my sacred self-love journey began, I was reading a spiritually based business book, *Attracting Perfect Customers*, by Jan Stringer. Intrigued by her attraction plan process, I engaged in a session with her. Before our meeting, she asked me to come prepared with a tabletop easel pad and multiple-colored markers.

Self-Acknowledgment

When it came time for our session, she had me start with her "leaving a legacy" process. This process has you identify the past contributions you have made and envision future contributions you intend to make that will in turn leave a lasting impact on others, long after you leave this world. She had me write these words on the top of my first poster page: What would you like to acknowledge yourself for?

Confused by her directions, I repeated them back to her. "What would I like to acknowledge myself for?" I asked.

She explained that most human beings look for validation outside themselves, which always leaves them unfulfilled and outwardly focused. She encouraged me to just follow the process and see what it produced for me upon completion. She gave me two hours to stay engaged in the question "What would I like to acknowledge myself for?" She specified that I begin each sentence with: "I acknowledge myself for _____and fill in the blank. Then she and I would talk after the two hours had passed.

It was slow going at first. I was self-removed as I began writing basic achievements as if I were listing bullet points on my resume. An hour and forty minutes were left ticking on the clock. I noticed I was shifting in my chair, stalling by picking up different colored markers while I dealt with the discomfort of acknowledging myself for my accomplishments.

Then it occurred to me to detail out the contributions I had made to my employers, former bosses, colleagues, and employees. I documented the contributions I had made to my social communities, places where I had volunteered, my women's advocacy efforts, and the charities and political campaigns where I made financial donations. There was an hour and fifteen minutes left on the clock, and it began to come easier.

I moved to yet a deeper level when I focused on the people in my personal life as I began to acknowledge myself for who I was and the impact I had made in my family's and friend's lives. I wrote out the specifics as they related to my mom, dad, grandmother, brothers, sister, and each of my friends.

An even deeper layer emerged as I acknowledged myself for the type of mother I had been through every stage of my daughter's life and who I was committed to being for my daughter in the future as we evolved.

Just when I thought I could go no deeper, I got to the core of the exercise. I was acknowledging myself for daring to find my voice and take a stand for my skills and talents. I was acknowledging myself for having the audacity to live my life differently when others wanted to keep me in their box so they could be comfortable. I acknowledged myself for having the internal strength to be present and available for others when they faced life-threatening illnesses

136

or in their dark times of tragic loss. I acknowledged myself for being true to my soul's purpose and my ability to take courageous action in the face of no agreement versus succumbing to others' opinions about how I should live or parent.

No other person could ever be aware of my contributions in all the domains of my life, just as no one can ever know your story better than you. There was no way that anyone else could acknowledge me for these things. If I kept looking outside myself for validation or seeking externally for someone to praise or acknowledge me for my contributions, it would have always fallen short, come up empty, or void of experiencing the fullness of my gifts, successes, and contributions to others.

Looking for or expecting someone else to value me would never have produced the results I gained from this exercise in self-acknowledgment. I could see where I had been dismissive or modest about my contributions, swept them under a rug, or given the credit to other people as women often do. This exercise brought a full appreciation of me to my conscious awareness as if for the first time the complete truth had been told, and it left me valuing my whole self in an honest and healthy way.

I can't encourage you enough to do this for yourself, for your heart, for your soul's deepest truth telling.

If you want to take this a step further, get a group of trusted friends together where you each have your own set of markers and a tabletop poster-size easel. Then give one another the gift of two or more self-acknowledgment writing hours. When you are done acknowledging yourself and all of your accomplishments and contributions are written on your pages, put everyone's name on individual pieces of paper in a bowl. Then take turns picking names out of the bowl until everyone has a partner. Then pair off into teams of two and have the one with the shortest hair go first. The one with the shortest hair will read hers out loud to her partner while her partner gives her full attention listening to the tremendously amazing and courageous woman sitting across from her. After the woman with the shortest hair completes all of hers, switch partners and repeat.

Keep tissues close by as this exercise promises to open hearts and deepen relationships with your friends but more importantly strengthen your relationship with yourself. If you choose this gift of self-acknowledgment, you can literally transform your relationship to yourself. It is the ability to own what's true about you, and you are worth every minute! How can you attract or create an honest relationship with someone else if you can't or are not willing to see the truth about yourself? Seeing and being who you truly are will foster a foundation that attracts others who will be able to see and acknowledge the same depth and truth about you too.

Self-Awareness

Several philosophers have weighed in on the topic of self-awareness. Chinese philosopher Lao Tzu said, "Mastering yourself is true power." Socrates is attributed with declaring that the unexamined life is not worth living, and he is quoted as stating, "Know thyself."

I got curious about how I could better know myself through the process of examining my life. I had taken off a year to give my heart a break, refuel, and recharge, so I had the time to spend on conscious reflection.

I was inspired to review my past relationships and behaviors. I wasn't sure what I knew, what I didn't know, and what I still had to learn. What I felt deep inside was that if I *did not* continue my self-love journey, I would risk *not* uncovering potential destructive relationship behaviors. If I skipped this opportunity to bring them to my awareness, I could sabotage the very thing I wanted, which was a true match for me and love relationship partner.

I kept envisioning two timelines in my mind. One timeline would be dedicated to condensing the prominent influencer characteristics

I had been exposed to in my early formative years. The second timeline would be the major intimate relationships I had attracted and chosen.

On my *Major Influencers Timeline*, I could see multiple personality characteristics I had gained from my major family influencers, including the ability to pioneer new ideas, always owning my own home, over-responsibility, being hard on myself, attention to detail, handling the chores, attracting men who were the baby of the family, being financially independent, and my absolute determination.

Having these insights into my major personality traits was invaluable. The one that resonated the most for me was my sense of over-responsibility. I could see where this one personality trait drained me in both my career and my personal relationships. over-responsibility, coupled with my underdeveloped skills in asking for what I want or need, contributed toward my inability to bring the best partner in me to a partnership with another person.

Major Influencers Timeline

Mother was the oldest child in her family often faced with traumatic and adult decisions. At a young age developed a sense of over-responsibility for things that she, objectively, should not have been responsible for; like the needs of her parents and her younger sibling. Basically, a single mother of 4 while dad was traveling for work long periods of time. Woman of many talents who wanted to and offered to go to work. Dad bought into the societal beliefs that a man had to be the breadwinner and the woman should assume the at home caretaker role. Ensured stability for her 4 children, moved into the workforce after dad moved out creating a beautiful life for herself doing what she loves. Unconditionally loving and loved by more people than I can count.

My age — 5 years old — 12 years old — 16 years old

Grandmother had a general disdain for men. She experienced men who treated her poorly in private and lovingly in public, putting on a show for others. She noted that she could not stay with a man whom she did not respect or who did not respect her. She experienced 2 divorces, lost two of her homes, stating always own your own home so that you can throw them out. Pioneer in her days, lived her life true to herself and did not live her life based upon the opinions of others.

Dad was the youngest of 7 boys, the baby of his family. Contracted polio before age 2 with no cure in sight. In a wheelchair, sustained continuous verbal abuse from other children and adults. With his sheer determination taught himself to walk, play chess, electrical engineering, and multiple instruments. A lifetime of external and internal criticism, coupled with his unrealized music career dreams, suffered from depression and alcoholism. Physically, verbally, and mentally abused my older brother and myself. Moved out when I was 16 and continued his financial support.

On my *Self-Awareness Timeline/Major Intimate Relationships*, I could see my own personal and relationship evolution. I laid out my age, where I was in my thinking and emotional development, and the men I was attracting and attracted to.

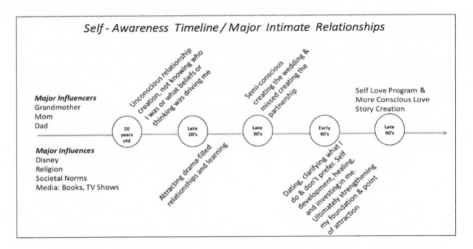

As I reflected on my timeline, more insights came to my awareness. I could see my journey from unconscious relationship creation to semiconscious relationship creation. I could see my evolution where I gained more awareness in my relationships and more consciously matured my skills so I could bring a better me to the relationships and more consciously create my love story.

I could see the journey was never a solitary one. A love story involves being willing to give and receive love. It takes engaging in relationship with another human being. Every man I dated or married had contributed to my collective love story just as I had contributed to theirs.

From my timeline vantage point, every one of them was my soulmate. They caused me to think about things I had not considered, have new insights, and engage in more fun and play. They caused my soul to expand its capacity to love, to feel deeper than I had ever felt, value myself, and expand my capacity to unconditionally love others.

They had each given me the gift of their love and even though some of the relationships were painful at the time, I was able to see them from my soul's point of view and appreciate each one of them for their love and contributions to this relationship road of imperfect perfection.

With the ability to look at both my *Major Influencers* and *Major Intimate Relationships*, I knew that my past relationship gift giving was not over. When you look at your *Major Influencers* and *Major Intimate Relationships*, most likely different insights will emerge for you, but what mine revealed to me was my sense of over-responsibility and hyper-independence. It was easy for me to see how these personality traits had impaired my ability to co-create meaningful partner relationships.

So, what's next? What's a woman to do with this information?

On your self-love path, your personal insights and inspired next steps or actions will be revealed to you in perfect timing, just as mine were to me. Curious and intrigued by the bigger picture unveiled to me when I created my life-to-date timeline and examined my major family influencers, I was inspired to look beyond what I could see on my timelines. I had learned about a very gifted clairvoyant in San Francisco, and one of his services was soul journey readings. I scheduled an appointment with him to see if I could gain even more understanding or insight into what else I needed to learn about myself.

The day came for my soul reading. I had never met this man or talked with him before. He asked me for my full name and birthdate. He was still for a few moments and then began walking me through the following story:

It is snowing heavily outside and bitterly cold. You are downtown, standing on one of the four corners of a moderately busy street. Across the street, a bus arrives. It stops at the bus stop, and opens its doors, allowing passengers to disembark or climb aboard. You see an elderly woman slowly get off the bus managing each step to ensure she does not fall. She begins to put on her gloves and drops one of them in the snow.

Then he stopped the story and asked me, "What do you want to do?" I replied, "Run across the street and help her." He noted that he wanted me to stay on my side of the street and continue to watch. Then he continued the story.

The elderly woman bends over to get the glove and instead of pulling it out of the snow, she buries it further below, making it harder to retrieve. She rubs her one glove and exposed hand together trying to create friction and keep her shaking hands warm. She is teetering a bit as she struggles to balance, bending over to dig deeper in the piling snow.

Then he stopped the story and asked me, "What do you want to do?" I replied, "Run across the street, dig out her glove, and help her." He noted that he wanted me to continue to hold myself back from "helping." Even though I know he is telling me a story, I am literally experiencing my anguish and angst over this hypothetical elderly woman who I can't go rescue. Then he continued the story, urging me to stay on my side of the street and keep watching.

The elderly woman shifts her body, working her way to get as close to the snow-covered ground so she can dig her glove out. She looks around her side of the street to see if someone is coming her way. She keeps shivering as the wind keeps blowing more snow on top of her glove buried beneath.

Then he stopped the story and asked me, "What do you want to do?" At this point in time, it is all I can do to keep myself from bolting across the street to take care of the old woman. I told him exactly how I was feeling inside. He noted that he wanted me to continue to stay on my side of the street and hold myself back from "helping." Then he urged me to keep watching.

The elderly woman painfully rooted around in the snow and was still unable to recover the second glove so she could place it back on her hand. She finally gave up her struggle and turned to walk back to the corner. She crossed the street and went into the store where she had long been eyeing a pair of leather cashmere-lined gloves for several months now. The elderly woman emerged from the store beaming as she walked out of the doorway having finally made this purchase for herself. As she walked away from the store, she disposed of her remaining old glove into the trash bin just outside of the building, happily walking to her destination with her warm hands wrapped in beautiful gloves.

A homeless woman, sitting inside a building entryway on the other corner of the street had been watching the unfolding scene intensely. She appeared seemingly out of nowhere, plucked the one glove out of the trash can then crossed the street and dug the other glove out of the snow. She placed both gloves on her hands as she needed them to keep her warm.

Then he spoke with compassion and gently pointed out that I, *in my spiritual arrogance*, think that I know better what other people need, think that I know what's better for them when I rush in to "help" or do things for them that they are completely capable of doing for themselves.

He was undeniably right, and every cell in my body knew it. I had just listened to a story—a story, mind you—and it fatigued me to stop myself emotionally and physically from going across the street to help the elderly woman. My mind began to race back over my relationships with family, friends, and men from my past. Where had I been a disabling friend, family member, or romantic partner by not staying on my side of the street?

It was extremely clear that had I stepped in and "helped" that elderly woman, she would not have experienced the joy and richness of owning a pair of cashmere-lined leather gloves and the homeless woman would not have known the warmth of those gloves left behind that she was able to retrieve. Where else might I have prohibited someone else's full experience or soul expansion because I stepped in uninvited?

Then he spoke again with compassion and noted that my soul's expansion this lifetime was to *learn how to not do anything for others unless I was asked*. What? Did I hear him accurately? Not do anything ... for anyone ... unless they asked? That comment flew in the face of anything and everything that I had ever been taught. I absolutely had no idea how to go about this and was not even sure it would be possible for me to realize.

Then he gave me real examples of how to go about this in everyday life, staying on my side of the street. He suggested the following:

1. Should someone drop something, don't pick it up unless they ask for your help.
2. Should you see someone doing something differently than how you would go about doing it, do not offer your opinion unless they ask for it—this is their life to live, not yours.
3. Should you see someone struggling financially, don't give them money to "bail" them out unless they ask for funds—then look to see if you can afford their request without compromising your own financial stability.
4. When you are at your job, do the work in your area. Avoid picking up the perceived slack of other colleagues. If you want to take on more responsibility, go to your boss and make a request for the opportunity to take on additional growth or development work.
5. When someone does ask for your help and they are not clear in their request, ask them how you can best support them. This will help you to *not* overreach and take on more than is yours to do.

My assignment was clear. It was obvious to me that my over-responsibility habit would be tempered, and I would take less on my shoulders by following the soul reading guidance. If I could allow others to have their own experience more fully, I would develop myself into a better friend, a more loving family member, and a more equal partner.

Self-Compassion

When you invest your energy in becoming more self-aware, personality traits that are ready to be upgraded will come to your realization. Along with these revelations is a wonderful opportunity to bathe yourself with compassion. Think about the compassion you have extended to other human beings and the empathy you have exhibited toward your best or closest friends. Self-compassion is taking those compassionate qualities and focusing them on you. In other words, being kind to yourself.

After digesting my over-responsibility personality traits revealed during my soul reading, I could have grabbed a solid wood two-by-fourand beat myself up with it for not knowing that about myself earlier in life. I am sure that a few men along the way wish I would have known it too. While I was creating my self-awareness timeline and reviewing my major intimate relationships, I could have spent quite a bit of time abusing myself with criticism and negative self-talk.

I could have spent my time comparing myself to other women. I have noticed that when I engage in comparing myself to others, it is another form of self-judgment in that I either judge myself as better off than the other person or judge myself worse off. This type of self-judgment bears no good fruit. I either fabricate a "win for me" at the expense of another woman or I fabricate a "loss for me" at the expense of myself. Self-judgment further solidifies the thinking that I am not enough or come up short in some area of my life. Spoiler alert! Self-judgment produces nothing good. It bears repeating: Self-judgment produces nothing good. I had to quickly get out of that self-critical bad neighborhood called my head and get into my heart center and embrace self-compassion.

Like so many women, I was naturally compassionate toward other people, but when the going got tough, too often I was toughest on myself. If my best friend was sharing her faults with me, of course, I would show her compassion. I knew that if I gave myself the same compassion that I extended to my best friend, I would attract people who would be compassionate toward me as well.

I learned how to develop a self-compassion practice. I practiced being kind to myself, embracing my humanity, and putting my flaws in perspective. It was a healthy way for me to love myself, be a better friend to myself, and energize forward movement. It looked like this:

- I am so glad that I am learning this now, and my life will get easier because of it.
- No one is perfect, and it is unrealistic for me to expect myself to be perfect.
- I am not alone in my personality trait. I bet there are other human beings on the planet who have experienced being overly responsible.
- I am the best person I have ever been, and I am right where I need to be right now.

If you are interested in exploring self-compassion, learning where you are in relationship to your self-compassion, and deepening your self-compassion practice, there is a free self-compassion test and more resources located at selfcompassion.org.

Self-Care

- How often have you made sure that everyone around you got taken care of first, then gave yourself the leftovers, that is, if anything was left over?
- Were you raised to think of others before yourself?
- Do you work a job or live a life that has you caretaking or caregiving to others?
- Have you been a parent or taken care of your parents, grandparents, or siblings?
- Do you now or have you worked two or more jobs just to make ends meet?
- Does your job have an undrainable lake of work waiting for you that you feel compelled or obligated to continually address?

Any of these life events could easily create an environment in which you are positioned to give everything you have to others leaving nothing left for yourself.

Self-Maintenance

There have been a few extended periods of time in my life when I put work and/or everyone else first and gave myself the leftovers or nothing. When I did this, I ended up so depleted that I had no idea if I could make it back. Choosing myself first became an act of survival. I was able to get myself back by starting with the self-maintenance basics:

- **Breathing** and slowing myself and my heartbeat down by closing my eyes and taking a handful of deep breaths every hour
- **Eating** nutritious foods that gave me energy
- **Sleeping** and allowing myself to rest and recover
- **Drinking** water to stay hydrated so my body and cells worked properly

Just starting with these four, building a habit first, and then seeing what I was ready to embrace next is how I managed to get myself back to the basics and improve my physical health.

Have you heard the phrase "Choose You"? Do you have the habit of putting yourself on the top of your to-do list? What would your life look like if you consciously chose to promote your own physical, mental, emotional, and spiritual well-being?

I created a list of my other physical needs, including my body, the home I lived in, and my vehicle. I made a deal with myself to choose myself by taking care of one item per week. I began by scheduling an eye appointment one week and then scheduling an oil change the next. Each week I crossed another item off my list and built the habit of investing in my overall physical stability.

The reason I started with self-maintenance activities was so I could create the distinction between foundational habits I had put in place earlier in my life to ensure my physical well-being from the self-care activities I was now engaged in during this "giving my heart a break" time of my life.

Self-Capacity Expansion

I was interested in seeing where caring more about myself would take me. I was interested in exploring my likes and dislikes. I was interested in seeing just how good I could feel by engaging in the adventure of dating myself. What was my capacity for joy? How much fun and joy could I allow myself to have? There is nothing more attractive than a happy woman in love with her own life. What would cause me to fall in love with myself and my life?

I love live music, and I lived in the Motor City where Motown Records got its start. I searched for live music venues and took myself out to listen, dance, clap, and sing. I followed my favorite artists to see where they might be playing, then bought tickets for my daughter and me to experience Elton John and then Madonna.

I had never really been a fan of watching television, so I turned in the cable box and saved myself the monthly fees. I loved to read. I skimmed the popular book lists and replaced TV time with mind-expanding books.

I lived on a golf course, so I purchased a starter set of golf clubs and expanded my golf game learning. My mother had been a solid golfer for years. This opened a new door to a mother-daughter activity where my mother and I got to enjoy playing the game together on many beautiful golf courses and meeting lots of wonderful people. I enjoyed the peace and beauty of living on the golf course. My townhouse was located on the seventh hole of the course. The golfers had to tee up on the other side of a rather large body of water and shoot across to reach the green. The flag on the green was approximately fifty feet from my back deck. I would frequently relax on the deck and enjoy watching the groups of friends or parents with their children navigate the hole much to my amusement.

I loved to travel and took myself on a cruise to explore a few Caribbean islands I had not yet seen. I had a beautiful home and I loved to entertain. I also loved my work and the team that reported to me. I had the time to develop friendships with three amazing women over this year of self-love.

The holiday season was in full swing with just three weeks to go before ringing in the new year and celebrating new beginnings.

After giving my heart a yearlong break, I wondered, *What would my new beginning be?*

Would I continue the path of loving my life as a single woman or explore another opportunity to love my life with a partner?

Introspection Questions

1. What does your sacred self-love program encompass? Does it include aspects of mental, physical, emotional, and spiritual well-being? How can you arrange your life or what might you ask of others so they can support you in taking care of your needs?

2. Are you willing to acknowledge yourself? If not, why not? What might be in the way of you owning the truth of who you are and what you contribute to others just by being you? What thoughts are you thinking that might be prohibiting you?

3. When will you be able to give yourself the gift of several hours of self-acknowledgment? Are you willing to add daily gratitude for self and self-acknowledgment to your sacred self-love program?

4. What does your Major Influencers Timeline look like? When you see the bigger picture, what do you see? What would your friends see if you showed it to them?

5. What does your Major Intimate Relationships Timeline look like? When you see the bigger picture, what do you see? What would your friends or family see if you showed it to them?

6. Looking at several of your past and present family and dating relationships, where might you have been over responsible or had a difficult time staying on your side of the street?

CHAPTER 12

TRUTH SERUM

There were only five days remaining before it would be time to open a bottle of my favorite champagne and ring in the new year by celebrating the previous year's accomplishments and toasting the next year's dreams and visions.

I have always loved the week after Christmas. I use this time to turn my attention toward releasing the old and consciously creating space for the new. I have always found it to be a freeing experience when I physically clean out and organize my closets and cupboards. While I pack the items to give away, I thank them for having supported me and I ask them to bless the next person or family that will receive them as I pay them forward.

Out with the old and in with the new also includes mentally or emotionally releasing old ideas and old thinking that no longer serves me. Another way I get ready to ring in each new year and prepare myself for attracting new experiences into my life is by creating and participating in a Burning Bowl ceremony. This is where I meditate and ask the question, "What habits, behaviors, limiting beliefs, or negative thinking no longer serves me?" Each time I ask the question, I write the answer on a small piece of paper and set it to the side. Then I ask the question again, repeating the process.

Once I have completed writing down what I am ready to release, one by one I intentionally throw them into the fireplace or my firepit and bless each one by thanking them for serving me thus far. Then I ceremoniously declare, "I release you and let you go to your highest good and I ask that you release me and let me go to my highest good."

I have formed the habit of clearing my physical, mental, and emotional spaces during this last week of the calendar year. This last week affords me plenty of time to mindfully engage in my rituals and complete them before early evening on December 31st. I do this intentionally so that I have a fresh canvas to create on for the upcoming year.

I have also formed the habit of acknowledging what I am grateful for over the past year. I call this my *Appreciation of This Past Year Ritual,* and it encompasses my appreciation of the new relationships I have developed, new insights gained, and my achievements. I wrote about several elements of self-love in the last chapter, including self-acknowledgment and self-care. The way I embraced these two self-love actions in my ritual this particular December 31st was to:

- Purchase a bottle of Veuve Clicquot champagne made by the French at their Champagne house founded in 1772, based in Reims, France
- Review and celebrate the year's new or completed relationships, contributions made to others or me, personal and professional accomplishments, internal or external growth and expansion, and the simple joy-filled experiences along the way

During my ritual I wrote each appreciation on a piece of paper and as I enjoyed reliving each relationship, accomplishment, experience, and memory, I toasted each one with pleasure and then set them to the side. When the fullness of my gratitude and appreciation for the previous year was achieved, I released all of them into my fireplace, ceremoniously declaring, "The Better It Gets, The Better It Gets" in delightful anticipation of what the next year would bring.

What a delightful way to spend my New Year's Eve! I was filled with gratitude, my loving cat, Cozmo, by my side, sipping champagne, and watching New York City's sparkling Waterford crystal ball make its descent during the countdown, signaling the passage of time.

Becoming Partnership Material

For me personally, this passage of time was completing the year of giving my heart a break, making an investment in *leveling up* me. My higher self knew that I needed to be and love my best self, first and foremost, before I could attract the partner and partnership I desired.

My higher self knew that experiencing the truth about me through self-acknowledgment would allow me to be more authentically myself, reduce my need for outside validation, and lessen my attention on the opinions of others so I could be a better partner in any relationship.

My higher self knew that by becoming aware of my inclination to be over-responsible, I would avoid the tendency to mother or overreach. By staying on my side of the street and honoring my partners' choices, I was better prepared to co-create a relationship on equal ground.

My higher self knew that by developing more self-compassion, it would allow me to equally treat myself with the same warmth, caring, and kindness that I extend to my partner, maintaining my balance and not allowing myself to diminish inside of any relationship.

My higher self knew that by habit-izing my self-care, it would be the gift that keeps on giving. When I invest in my health—physically, mentally, emotionally, financially, and spiritually—it would naturally contribute to my overall happiness, reduce my stress, and enable me to bring the best of myself to my relationships.

My higher self was literally guiding me in raising my vibration so that I would be the point of attraction for that which I wanted to attract.

Components of Creation and Attraction

In my teenage years, I was introduced to various components of creation when I learned about the power of positive thinking, the laws of prosperity, and the use of affirmations.

Toward the very end of my twenties, I read the book *Creative Visualization* by Shakti Gawain. She taught me about getting still and connecting deeply to my inner knowing. When I did the exercises in her book, it accelerated the development of my intuition and increased my abilities to creatively visualize that which I wanted to manifest in my life.

In 1993, I began facilitating others in manifesting the things or improved situations they wanted for their lives. I supported one woman in attracting the best employees for her division, another woman in seeing a costly lawsuit dropped against her company and the valued customer relationship restored, and another woman manifest her dream job, including a 30 percent salary increase.

In 1995, I recorded a guided imagery meditation titled *You Are the Light of the World*. The meditation is designed to enable the participants to take their highest vibration and consciously amp up their broadcast frequency and transmission signal, much like a lighthouse or continuous messaging beam of light.

Over the years I have created and attracted homes, cars, luxury trips, stellar mentors and coaches, women's conferences, and the experience of a lifetime dream job overseas for myself and my daughter, including her Mary Poppins-like nanny.

Could I apply all the things I had learned over the years and consciously create and attract my perfect partner and partnership?

When it came to matters of the heart, doubt about my creation abilities had crept in after setting my powerful intention and semiconsciously attracting **Mr. Childlike.** This is where I created the marriage before cultivating the partnership resulting in a second divorce and me quickly learning that I can alter my life by simply deciding to choose the path of joy.

Could I try creating a relationship again knowing that I was wiser and more conscious in my creations since that experience?

Was my leveling up over the last year enough to prepare myself to win my gold medal in the game of love?

One very important thing I had learned about myself because of all my relationship experiences was that I was no longer willing to unconsciously fall in love.

Conscious Creation

Some women have written love letters to the future husbands and partners they hope to encounter. You can read these letters on the internet. In some of them, they write: *"Someday I will meet you."* and they express their soul's longing proclaiming, *"I miss you even though I haven't met you yet."* These letters are well intended yet stay focused on the *someday in the future or the absence* of their beloved. This type of thinking creates a resistance to that which you want to attract. It is so slight that you might not even hear the difference or catch it.

Some women have created dream boards, vision boards, or some form of pictorial display of things they would like to manifest in their lives. Some have developed physical displays using poster boards, closet doors, or walls, and some have developed online displays using tools like Canva or Pinterest.

Whether physical or virtual, these pictorial reminders of your goals and dreams can be attracting or repelling your desires.

When you see these daily reminders, are you basking in the joy of having them, tasting them, touching them, feeling them, and reveling in the joy of them, or are you unintentionally looking at them through the eyes of deprivation and limiting thoughts of not holding or having them?

When these displays are viewed with the feeling and thinking of "I already have" or "I already am," inspired ideas and actions will naturally arise. When inspiration comes, it is important to take or engage in the inspired action(s), as they are moving you into the future you are creatively envisioning.

As a more conscious creator, I wanted to purposely focus my attention and intention, in alignment with my desires, to create and attract the partner and partnership perfect for me. After investing a year of time in myself, I was standing on a new foundation for creating and I was inspired to create a vision book and write out my love story.

Using my intuition, I asked for the location of the right journal filled with blank pages for my love story writing. My intuition guided me to a Barnes & Noble bookstore, which saved me from going to Staples, Target, Hallmark, and spending hours searching for a journal at the local mall. When I arrived at Barnes & Noble,

it did not even take five minutes; the journal almost jumped off the shelf and into my hands more than sixteen years ago. When you look at the picture, you may be able to see how it has been held and love-worn.

Much to my delight, the inside cover had the word *DESIRE* on it and the word *DESIRE* was sprinkled throughout multiple pages inside of the journal. This lined up perfectly with my attention and intention, in alignment with my desires, to create and attract the partner and partnership perfect for me. I enjoyed the ornate arrow on the front cover of the journal and the more whimsical arrow on the inside cover.

The arrows reminded me of Cupid's arrow. According to mythology, Venus is the goddess of love and beauty, and Cupid, the god of affection, is her son. As legend would have it, Cupid shoots magical gold- tipped arrows, causing humans to deeply love. What a delightful, playful thought to have when looking at this image.

With my perfect journal in hand, I walked over to the other side of the bookstore where a myriad of magazines was displayed. My intention was to acquire inspiring pictures and words or phrases that would stimulate feelings and evoke emotions in alignment with my desire to create and attract the perfect partner and partnership for me.

Once again, to save me from flipping through each one, I sat down on a bench close to the magazine display, closed my eyes, then asked my intuition which ones I should pick up. When I opened my eyes, I paid particular attention to the ones that stood out as if they were being presented to me. I ended up with travel, entertainment, relationship, and finance magazines. My magazine collection from this bookstore was completed with the inspiration that you can always find in a copy of O, *The Oprah Magazine*.

I left the bookstore and went to a grocery store and then a drugstore where I repeated my intuitive process as I viewed their racks of magazines. I purchased the ones that called to me until I felt satisfied that I had plenty of magazines to artfully use in my partnership creation and went home.

I love how music can be used to energize, calm, enhance productivity, or encourage creativity. I feel the most creative when I am listening to light piano or classical music, so I turned on my tunes to set the mood and relaxed in my comfy oversized chair for two.

With the pile of magazines to my right and a recycling bag waiting to catch the leftovers, I was ready to rapidly remove pictures and words releasing them from the seams of these magazines for a grander purpose. This was not a job for my analytical mind that would get in the way by evaluating and debating each image. This was a mission for my senses, my visual and emotional skills, which know in a flash if something is resonant and feels right or does not.

I took the magazines one by one and turned their pages quickly, observing what caught my eye and stirred my emotions. If a picture spoke to my heart and desires, I took out the page and placed it on my left. If a word or phrase sparkled, inspired, and grabbed my attention, I took out the page and placed it on my left. As the recycling bag on my right filled up with magazine remnants, the pile on my left grew with inspiration and my heart's desire. When I dropped the last magazine into the recycling bag, I noticed I was filled with optimistic expectations. What a great way to spend the day, end the evening, and go to sleep.

I began the next morning looking through the stack of inspirational phrases and images. They caused me to wonder what I should call this man. What is his name? I played with several names in my mind, wrote them on paper, and said them out loud just to hear their sound as they rolled off my tongue. Then it clicked into place and resonated deeply, I would call him my *Eternal Divine Partner (EDP)*.

Eternal Divine Partner was the perfect description for him. I wanted a man who was not only interested in exploring the physicalness of this planet but was also interested in continuous expansion and exploration of his spirituality and higher self. I wanted a man who stood firmly on his own foundation and desired to have an equal partner. I wanted a man who wanted to grow together with me co-creating our relationship and future experiences.

Now that this man had a name, what other characteristics would be embodied in my *Eternal Divine Partner*?

*This part of the creative process yields much better results and outcomes when you know **what you want** to attract. With almost 4 billion men on the planet, you could attract every kind of man anywhere across the globe without appropriate search filters. Clarity and specificity matter! It's your love story and your creation; what do you like, love, want, must have, and desire?*

This is where all the boyfriends or husbands from your past have served you well. Reflect on the men from your past. Write down what you preferred and did not prefer about their individual characteristics by answering the Introspection Questions at the end of Chapter 8.

Because I had already identified what I appreciated and learned from each of the men in my past, I began writing down my non-negotiables in an affirmative fashion.

Non-negotiables are characteristics, qualities, or capabilities that are not up for discussion. If you were buying a car, wheels, doors, and windows would be non-negotiable characteristics. Leather seats and Bose speakers might be non-negotiable qualities. A backup camera or navigational guidance system might be non-negotiable capabilities.

Here are several examples of characteristics, qualities, and capabilities I felt were non-negotiable for me:

- He has deep compassion and a heart filled with love that he generously shares with me, my daughter, and others.
- He is a single heterosexual male, completely available, desires a relationship and to be in a committed powerful conscious partnership with me.
- He accepts and adores my daughter, treats her like she is his own, and she is equally as comfortable with him.
- If he has children, they are grown and want their father to be satisfied and happy. They love, adore, and accept me and I love, adore, and accept them.
- He is passionate and sexually attractive and monogamous with me and intimate with only me.
- He is intelligent, bright, and inquiring.
- He is spiritually aware and intuitive.
- He takes care of his well-being and works out several times per week.
- He is fun to be with, playful, and makes me laugh.
- He loves and appreciates all kinds of music.
- He is adventurous and loves to travel with me.
- He honors and respects women, especially me.

- He is smoke and addiction free.
- He has a high degree of personal integrity.
- He is clean and organized.

Writing down your non-negotiables brings greater clarity to what you want to attract. Non-negotiables are a portion of your vision, and you want to create the whole picture. This is where all the relationships from your past have served you. *They have assisted you in getting clearer about the experiences you desire or experiences you do not desire.*

Reflect on the relationships from your past. Write down what you preferred and did not prefer about the relationship. What worked and what did not work about the relationship? What are the things you want to ensure are part of your next-level-up relationship creation?

I began writing down my desired relationship characteristics in an affirmative fashion. Here are several examples of items that I felt were important for the partnership match I was creating:

- We genuinely enjoy each other and are happy just holding hands and hanging out together.
- We are energetically matched to each other.
- Together we enjoy live entertainment, movies, and traveling to new places.
- We value each other's input, talents, and contributions.
- We learn from each other.
- We are both open, honest, and deeply intimate with each other.
- We create a safe and nurturing place in our home for ourselves and others.
- We both are good listeners of each other, and we hear and see the best in each other always.
- We enjoy entertaining socially in our home.
- We are proud of each other and support each other's dreams and goals.
- We consciously co-create our future together.

When you are ready to create your next relationship, whether it be dating, committed, married, or divorced friends, there is always an opportunity to be more conscious by bringing the clarity of that which you want to the forefront.

Bringing It All Together

Inside my vision journal I created a predominant affirmation at the top of each creation page.

I have an eternal love affair with my divine partner,

and he has an eternal love affair with me.

Notice the grammatical tense of my now affirmation. It begins with *I have*. Notice that my now affirmation is bi-directional. Not only do I have, but he has too. I did not want to create a single-sided relationship. I wanted to be sure that we both had a part in the partnership.

I went through my stack of inspirational phrases and images. I identified the best of the best and cut them out of the pages that held them. One by one, I combined the most inspiring phrases with the most emotionally evoking images that were representational of and in alignment with my desires. I laid out various combinations in front of me until I was inspired by looking at them. Once I was pleased with a picture page layout, I took my glue stick in hand and attached the pictures and phrases to a page in my love story vision journal. Here are two of the original sixteen pages from my vision book:

After I completed gluing all my image and phrase designs to my love story journal pages, I used the lined pages in the journal and wrote down all the characteristics, qualities, and capabilities I desired in a partner and for our partnership. Each statement beginning with "He is" or "We are" or other positive affirming words describing the now state of his being or our relationship. I wrote over 120 positive affirming statements in my vision book. Here is one of the original pages:

165

I took prior relationships, gleaned the best from them, and used them as a catalyst to begin of the next foundation. I gathered images and phrases resonant with that which I wanted to create and incorporated them into the new foundation I was laying. I created a predominant vision statement and gave my man a name infusing the new foundation with more reality. I designed sixteen pages of inspiring images and described in detail what already was, writing over 120 positive statements laying the cornerstone in my new foundation. I brought it all together, and in my hands was my love story vision book and manifestation manuscript. *Now what?*

Whether it is a screenplay yearning to become a movie, floor plans desiring to become a house, or a blueprint intending to become a building, there are creators behind them. Having experienced the results of multiple manifestations over the years, *as a creator, I knew that I had to breathe life into my creation.*

How do you breathe life into something? For me, being alive is beyond going through the steps or motions of a process. Any robot or computer can be programmed to go through the steps or motions of a process. Being alive and breathing life into my creation meant engaging my heart, feelings, emotions, and all my senses to bring to life my **Eternal Divine Partner** and Partnership with gratitude and love.

It was still the first week of January. I made an agreement with myself to take time to breathe life into my love story vision book before going to bed. Each evening I got comfortable in my oversized chair, with my loving cat, Cozmo, by my side, and I opened my love story vision book. I placed my hand on every page, opened my heart, and filled them with love. I basked in the inspirational images of the two of us and loved that I have an eternal love affair with my divine partner and that he has an eternal love affair with me.

I savored every conscious creative statement about him and our relationship and loved knowing that my perfect match was attracting me just as I was attracting him. With every cell in my body, I was filled with gratitude as I reveled in the playful and passionate experiences the two of us were enjoying together.

I literally loved my evening ritual. It was peaceful and meditative. It brought me joy to contemplate and filled me with gratitude right before bedtime.

During the third week of February, I was inspired to join the Match.com dating site. I was also inspired to take the essence of my love story vision book and create a clear brief description of what I was looking for in a partner and partnership. This was my opportunity to be brave and present to the outer world an aligned and congruent view of my heartfelt desires.

Once I posted my brief and brilliant description on my new profile, the beauty of this inspired action was made clear. It created "gone guys" by repelling the men that were not a match for me while attracting noticeably different men than I had attracted in the past on dating sites.

During the last week of February, a man reached out, and it appeared that we had quite a bit in common. We began the usual emailing back and forth over several days, and then he asked if he could call me. It felt right, so I gave him my cell number.

On Friday evening, he had just wrapped up watching his son's basketball game and called me on his way back home. Like me, he had one child, had lived in multiple places working for different companies, owned his own home, was well-traveled, spiritually minded, and loved a wide variety of music. In fact, he had double majored in college obtaining degrees in economics and classical music history. We talked for almost three hours, and he asked me if I wanted to meet him for lunch the next day.

On Saturday, it was snowy and still very cold in Michigan. When I pulled into the restaurant parking lot, he was already outside of his vehicle leaning against the hood of his dark green Ford Mustang Bullitt. It's one of the most recognized cars in movie history, driven by Steve McQueen in the movie *Bullitt*, and as you might imagine, a very manly car designed with the power to drag race.

I stepped out of my metallic red, two-seater hard-top convertible wearing jeans, boots, and a leather jacket. Now we knew another thing about the two of us—we liked to have fun on the road, drive fast, and appreciate the craft of beautiful car design.

Neither one of us ordered a drink, but you would have thought someone slipped us truth serum. The level of honesty was refreshing, so much so that neither of us wanted to leave the conversation.

We talked again Sunday evening and agreed to meet early for coffee on Tuesday morning where the honesty continued. We both agreed that we wanted to take our profiles off the dating site and see where our truth-serum relationship might take us.

Our first date night arrived: dinner at my place on Wednesday. I prepared a salad and seasoned swordfish steaks for baking. Much to my surprise, he arrived bearing gifts. In his arms were a bottle of my favorite French champagne, flowers, and a chic silver box. While I arranged the flowers, he opened the bottle of champagne. Then he asked me to open the silver box. It contained two elegant champagne flutes cradled in silver satin. As he poured the bubbles into the fluted crystal, he said he had a feeling that we might be toasting many things together.

Since we were being honest, I shared with him my belief about the law of attraction. I talked a bit about the journey that led me

to create a love story vision journal for attracting my eternal divine partner. I handed him my vision book and let him read it. With his glass of champagne in hand, he turned the pages absorbing the information while I tended to the oven and plating dinner. When he finished reading my Consciously Created Love Story Journal, he was honest with me, stating that he met every line in the book, except two...

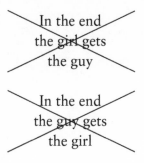

~~In the end the girl gets the guy~~

~~In the end the guy gets the girl~~

IN THE END
THEY CONSCIOUSLY CHOSE EACH OTHER
AND
IT WAS JUST THE BEGINNING ...

BONUS MATERIAL

Author's Note

"To find yourself, think for yourself."
— *Socrates*

Higher Self: Highlights

It's Your Love Story
You get to create it unconsciously or consciously, your choice.

It's Your Higher Self's Love Story
What would your most real self, choose for you?

It's Your Soul's Love Story
What does the essence of your very being know to be true for you?

Take the time to see the love everywhere around you.
Write about it in your daily gratitude journal until it permeates the air you breathe.

Get interested, curious, and ask questions about the motivations, desires, major influences, and fears of the main characters (significant family influencers) in your life.
Where have you unconsciously or consciously assumed their desires, fears, habits, or beliefs?
Where did they make you who you are today and where will you recreate or reshape yourself?
Get inquisitive and explore the significant influences in your life.
What beliefs do you hold dear?
What religious, spiritual, ethnic, and societal norms have you adopted?
Are they yours or someone else's?
Do they serve and support you?

See your love story comprehensively with new eyes and give yourself the gift of appreciating the love exchanged in every encounter past and present.

What did you and your higher self learn from each relationship encounter?

How did each relationship assist you in gaining greater clarity, expansion, or healing?

What new experiences were you afforded because of the time spent with each man?

How did you expand your abilities to be in a relationship?

What is the holistic love story your soul wants to share with you?

Level up yourself, embrace self-love, make room for yourself in your life, fall in love with every cell of your being, and cherish and steward the most amazing gift you have to offer others, YOU!

Acknowledge all your accomplishments, contributions, and rich character traits.

How can you improve the way you talk and think about yourself and embody more self-compassion?

What is your self-maintenance, self-care, self-expansion, and level-up plan?

Evolving Yourself

Loving yourself, becoming more self-aware, embodying self-compassion, and habit-izing self-care will enable you to bring a healthier you to every relationship you have.

Leveling up yourself will give you a new vantage point from which to attract your perfect partner.

Bringing a more complete version of Ms. or Mrs. Right to the relationship will empower you to create the next chapter of your love story more consciously.

Yours in Conscious Creation,

Heather Leah

For additional resources and opportunities to engage in the conversation, visit www.ConsciouslyCreateYourLoveStory.com and be on the lookout for book two of the Consciously Create Series, Retreats at the Winery, the Companion Journal, and Self-Love Program for leveling up YOU!

HelloPrenup: Consciously Create Your Financial Love Story
Julia Rodgers, Esq., CEO of HelloPrenup.com

Durable relationships include a strong dose of passion and excitement tempered with a heaping tablespoon of mindful deliberation. You know how some couples just sort of fall into each subsequent stage of a relationship without giving it much thought, while others carefully navigate each phase with a high degree of intentionality? Which way do you think is more likely to lead to a lasting, healthy relationship? If you guessed the second one, congratulations, you win a million dollars! Not really. But you just might win yourself something better: a close connection with a long-term partner.

If you're someone who values this mindful intentionality in relationships, you will probably approach marriage in much the same way. You'll likely tune into your feelings and experiences attentively in order to gradually assess whether a partner might be someone with whom you're compatible enough to consider marrying ... and you should absolutely approach your prenup in much the same way.

As a divorce attorney-turned-CEO and co-founder of a prenup platform, I have seen my fair share of relationship-ending miscommunication. In fact, this is precisely why I believe that all couples should consider a prenup prior to marriage, and in doing so, make conscious, intentional decisions on how they plan to manage their finances (and life!) as a married couple.

These days, prenups are not only for the wealthy and not only for those who have significant assets to protect. They're for anyone who wants to thoughtfully lay out plans and arrangements that will govern both their marriage and their contingency plan in case of divorce, offering them priceless peace of mind. Couples who do not elect to obtain a prenup are subject to a default prenup in the form of the laws of their particular state. Creating a prenup, then, is an integral part of consciously creating your love story by brainstorming supportive plans and putting your conscious agreements in writing well before you walk down the aisle.

The personalized prenup-generating software created by me and my co-founder is a women-owned startup called HelloPrenup, which allows couples to generate their own customized prenups for a fraction of the price and complication that typically goes into drafting a premarital contract. More importantly, the interactive and personalized nature of the platform guides couples through important issues they'll need to discuss, helping them to consciously co-create an agreement that will set the tone for their marriage.

In the service of consciously creating your own love story, let's discuss some important points of conversation. It is recommended to start talking about these topics as soon as possible. If you feel uncomfortable talking about some of these things, ask yourself why. The discomfort might just be an indicator that you really need to talk about them in order to transcend the tension they're causing by being left unspoken. Some of these topics may be uncomfortable for some couples but talking about them calmly and mindfully can bring your relationship to new levels of durability and understanding.

1. How will assets acquired after marriage be owned – jointly or separately?
Some couples prefer to keep assets and property that they acquire during marriage separate. They might consider this simpler or see it as a hallmark of their individuality within their union. Others like to classify everything acquired after marriage as marital property, sharing it all in the eyes of the law. Some couples choose to keep assets acquired before marriage as separate, and just the appreciation on those assets over the course of their marriage, as marital/community property. There is no right answer; your arrangement should depend entirely on what will be the best investment for your particular relationship going forward.

2. What about assets owned by each partner before the marriage? Which of these should remain separate, and which would you like to become marital property?

This question can require a lot of thought, especially as you consider various types of assets. For example, if one of you owns a business, you'll need to decide whether the other one can or should acquire any interest in that business or reap the benefits of any appreciation of the business. If either or both of you have received an inheritance or gifts of substantial value, what about those? What about inheritance? Should it remain separate or be merged into the marital estate? And what about income from your job, from investments, and from any other source? Should debt acquired prior to marriage be considered separate debt, or marital debt? These are just a few of the questions you'll need to consider when deciding which, if any, individual assets the two of you would like to remain separate after marriage.

3. Will you and your future spouse share a joint bank account or keep only your separate accounts?

You might prefer to allocate some funds to a joint bank account. Or all funds. Or no funds. The bank account conversation can also lead to a discussion of deeper questions about how money is to be allocated during the marriage. Will each of you be responsible for different shared expenses? If one spouse earns significantly more, will they sponsor a more substantial portion of some shared expenses? How will this be decided or renegotiated if conditions change further on down the line?

4. If you do eventually find that you've grown in different directions and decide to end your marriage, how will marital property be divided?

No one likes to talk about this, but the truth is that many marriages do end in divorce, and some people find growth through being in different relationships during different life phases and stages of their development. Consciously creating your relationship can drastically decrease the likelihood of divorce, but it could still happen and it's important to consider how marital property would be divided, just in case.

Marital property could be divided equally, it could be divided according to the amount each spouse contributed to each marital asset, or it could be divided according to what the state law dictates as a default. It is important to include a clause about this in your prenup because making a decision while you're level-headed and closely bonded is almost certainly more conducive to an amicable split than trying to decide when tensions are high or letting the laws of the state govern what happens to your property.

5. Should spousal support be awarded in the event of a divorce?

Spousal support, also known as alimony, means money paid regularly by one spouse to another after a divorce. Including a clause about spousal support in a prenuptial agreement is especially protective for women, because women often give up years of their careers and sacrifice their earning potential in order to stay home with kids. A provision for spousal support can protect a spouse who does this, or it can be beneficial in many other circumstances in which it makes sense for one partner to be entitled to payments from the other in case of divorce. The right to spousal support can be waived entirely in a prenup or waived only for the first few years of marriage. Alternatively, the couple can choose when they write their prenup to have the state they lived in at the time of marriage make decisions about spousal support or the state they live in at the time of divorce.

Again, there are no wrong answers to any one of these questions. Make sure you take the time to approach these issues with thoughtful deliberation. You should expect that you may not agree on everything, but imbuing the conversation with a sense of care, intentionality and compassion will help you to negotiate differences and reach compromises that you can both get behind, all the while strengthening your relationship and your ability to navigate challenging situations together.

These are only a few of the questions couples should discuss as they consciously co-create their prenuptial agreements. For a deeper dive into conscious prenup generation, check out HelloPrenup's platform, which presents these questions and more with a high degree of detail and a focus on collaboration.

Julia Rodgers is an attorney and the CEO *of HelloPrenup.com. She believes that open and honest discussion about finances is key to consciously creating a long-lasting love story. HelloPrenup is the premier online platform for creating a prenuptial agreement and has been featured on* Shark Tank, *in* Forbes, *GeekWire,* The Boston Globe, Lawyers Weekly, The American Bar Association Journal, *and The Knot, among others.*

Embracing Your Essence: Consciously Dressing in Alignment with Your Essence

Patsy Sanders

People make an assessment about you in the first five seconds they meet you, and 50 percent of that is based on how you are dressed. That's according to Harvard Business School.

Fair or not, appearances matter.
If you walk into a fine-dining restaurant and the staff attire is not clean and professional, you will doubt the quality of the food you'll be getting. If you meet someone, and you are not attracted to them, you might not make much of an effort to get to know them better.

If you're not dressing in alignment with your essence, you may not attract your ideal client, partner, or social connections, and you are missing out.

How one dresses in a professional setting should be congruent with their brand. The same is true in social settings. Your look should be congruent with who you are and what you want to communicate about yourself.

People aren't attracted to you unless you are attractive.
What does "attractive" really mean?

Attractiveness is how you present yourself overall.

Your style is a head-to-toe look that communicates a lot about you. It helps reveal your personality, character traits, values, and even your ethics. It reflects how you feel about yourself, highlights your essence, and expresses the nature of you. *It is not a name brand, size, or price tag. It is not what the fashion industry says.*

It is more than wearing nice clothes. It is wearing clothes that make you feel confident and comfortable and reveal a bit about who you are. Your appearance should draw people in; it is a bridge to connection. And all that happens in the first five seconds of people meeting you.

Dressing in Harmonic Alignment
When we get dressed, we want to be harmonically aligned with the clothes we wear.

Think of your clothes as the frame of a painting; they are supposed to highlight you as the masterpiece, not distract. Just as you would never put the *Mona Lisa* in a lime-green frame, you don't want to dress in clothes that draw more attention than the person wearing them. Knowing your best colors, textures, and fabrics will have people look at YOU first, then your outfit.

That's why it is so important to have a color palette and style that work for you. When you get it right your skin will glow, your eyes will sparkle, and YOU will be the center of attention. Not only that, but you will have a wardrobe that is much easier to mix and match. Dressing in the elements is about dressing to be who you were born to be, not whom the world says you should be. In your element, even people who have known you for a long time will notice you look amazing, they just won't know why, or exactly what you're doing differently, they just know they are more attracted to you.

I experienced this in my own life.
Years ago, I was trying to rebuild my business as a hairstylist and make new friends after moving to the Sonoma County wine country. It was a struggle for about four years. But then a friend invited me to do hair at a weekend retreat where she was doing style makeovers for her professional speaker clients. She believed that their being seen for who they were was critical for their success. The image stylist draped each client in different color fabrics. She looked at what colors had THEM look their best, made their eyes light up, their blemishes recede, and their skin look like they were wearing makeup when they weren't. Then she asked about their personality and their childhood traits, she looked at their

features and felt their skin. She was discerning which element (Air, Water, Earth, or Fire) each speaker was and teaching them how to embrace their essence. She then had me cut and style each person's hair according to their element.

After we were all done, my friend offered to color type me using the Elements Color Typing System.

I said, "No, I'm good." I thought I knew everything. After all, I had been color typed in the Seasonal Color Typing System as a "Winter" decades ago. Since then, I wore lots of black, jewel tones, and I even had some stylish purple highlights in my hair because that's what I had been told was right for me. I thought I looked okay, plus black was supposed to be slimming! (Little did I know it also made me invisible.)

"What if what you're wearing is keeping people from working with you?" my friend asked.

She explained that it went beyond just color and included energy, textures, tones, and patterns that would help me show up as approachable, confident, and attractive. I decided to take a chance. It turned out my element and essence were "Fire," which, initially, I resisted, but then we purchased a few tops and she encouraged me by saying, "Just try it and see what people say." Reluctantly, I agreed. I wanted to see if people would really interact with me differently.

The first day I wore one of the new tops, a client commented on how nice I looked. The second day someone else said I looked really pretty. Every day that I wore one of those tops I received compliments. By the second week, the salon owner asked me what I was doing because I looked so amazing lately. That was it. I was convinced! I was such a convert I became an essence image stylist, worked with my friend, and bought her business when she retired.

What I realized was that when I dressed in my element, people connected with me more easily; they finally saw ME. I was being attractive and easily attracted my ideal clients. My business took off. After forty years in business, I realized I'd been hiding in plain sight all that time.

3 Universal Tips Anyone Can Use to Look Their Best

When you don't yet know your element, here are three universal tips you can use right now to look your best.

1. **Universal colors:** Myth: Everyone looks good in black. Truth: Black is easy for everyone, but black is not good for everyone. Eggplant is your new black. Eggplant is a power color that everyone does look good in. Teal gets everyone seen and noticed. It's a dynamic color that will help you be remembered. If it is important to be powerful and approachable, wear eggplant. If it is important to be attractive and memorable, wear teal.

2. **What do you see first?** Look in a full-length mirror. Do you see you or your outfit first? You want people to see you first. When in doubt go with solid, medium-color tones. Accessorize with jewelry, a scarf, or wear a jacket to look more professional.

3. **From the shoulders up:** The eye naturally goes from the top down. The first thing people look at is your hair. A hairstyle and fresh cut show that you care about yourself. It is hard for your client to assume you'll care about them if you are not showing that you care about your own appearance. Too much makeup or no makeup at all will have you be unrelatable. A little mascara and lip color will help you look fresh and be seen.

Don't Hide in Plain Sight

If you don't make a good first impression, people move on. It will cost you both socially and professionally. If you look unapproachable it will make connecting that much tougher—if you are even noticed at all. Ultimately, if you select outfits that accentuate your most authentic, confident self, you will be much more likely to attract people who resonate with who you really are.

Consciously embracing your essence is an exhilarating and fun way for you to align your clothing style to your inner being so that you are expressing the entirety of you from head to toe and inside out.

Patsy Sanders
Patsy@EmbracingYourEssence.com
https://embracingyouressence.com

ABOUT THE AUTHOR

Heather Leah brings her leadership skills in organizational change, personal and professional development, and executive coaching to her work with women around the world. She has been featured in major media outlets, including radio, newspapers, and television. Heather is on a mission to shine a light on outdated relationship thinking and limiting beliefs with the goal of co-creating a world where every woman has a choice and a voice. Keep this in mind: There is nothing more attractive than a woman in love with her own life!

Heather is passionate about empowering women in their professional *and* personal lives. By sharing her experience, Heather intends to inspire and empower women by providing them with the tools they need to consciously create their love stories.

Heather lives in the Catoctin Mountains of Maryland, with her husband, Michael. Together they own Celebration Cellars Winery and Retreat Center, where they host events and create a relaxed yet elegant environment for their customers and guests.

Visit Heather's website, ConsciouslyCreateYourLoveStory. com, for additional products and services, including upcoming Consciously Create Your Love Story retreats held at the winery and other locations.